YADOOL

THE SACRED CIRCLE

BY MASTER HARTLEY

Printed and bound in the United States of America
First printing • ISBN # 978-0-9908913-4-5
Copyright © 2016

TO ORDER ADDITIONAL COPIES OF:

YADOOL

THE SACRED CIRCLE

BY MASTER HARTLEY

visit www.martialartstory.com

**Great appreciation and thanks to
Mr. Jacob Williams for his illustrations.**

SCOTT COMPANY PUBLISHING
P.O. Box 9707
Kalispell, MT 59904
Toll Free: 1-800-628-0212
Fax: 1-406-756-0098

This story is inspired by the
gifted and gallant young athletes
in the dojang of Big Sky Martial Arts.

TABLE OF CONTENTS

Legend to Map of Korean cities, ports, and temples sited in "Yadool".

1) Mt. Paektu   This sacred mountain in Korean lore straddles the Korean/Chinese border.

2) Sinuju   This village, at the foot of Mt. Paektu, is the home of Master Kija and his students.

3) Chanbaek Range   Northern mountain range in which lies Mt. Paektu and which Hyun Cho must cross.

4) Daegu   The large city where Jung sup Kim is to deliver *Il Jang* to the Buddhist, Woncheuk, in the Taigu Temple.

5) Port Sonjin   Hyun Cho steals a boat to follow the coast south.

6) Hungnam   This is the large port city in which Hyun Cho seeks the Jinheung Sanctuary.

7) SEOUL   Korea's largest city and capital.

8) Mt. Samgaksan   The Doseonsa Temple is located in the foothills of this mountain, near Seoul.

9) Island of Jeju, Port of Seogwipo   The port is the destination of Chin carrying *O Jang* Eui sook Chung, carrying *Sa Jang*.

10) Kwangtu   Train stop city for Eui sook and Chin Ho.

11) Mokpo   Coastal town where Deng Min took Euik sook and Chin Ho.

12) Port of Pohang   The port where Jung sup Kim meets the Taigu monk.

13) Pusan   Southern "gateway" to Korea where the Haedong Yonggung temple is located.

14) Gyeongbu Railroad   Japanese built railroad from Seoul to Pusan.

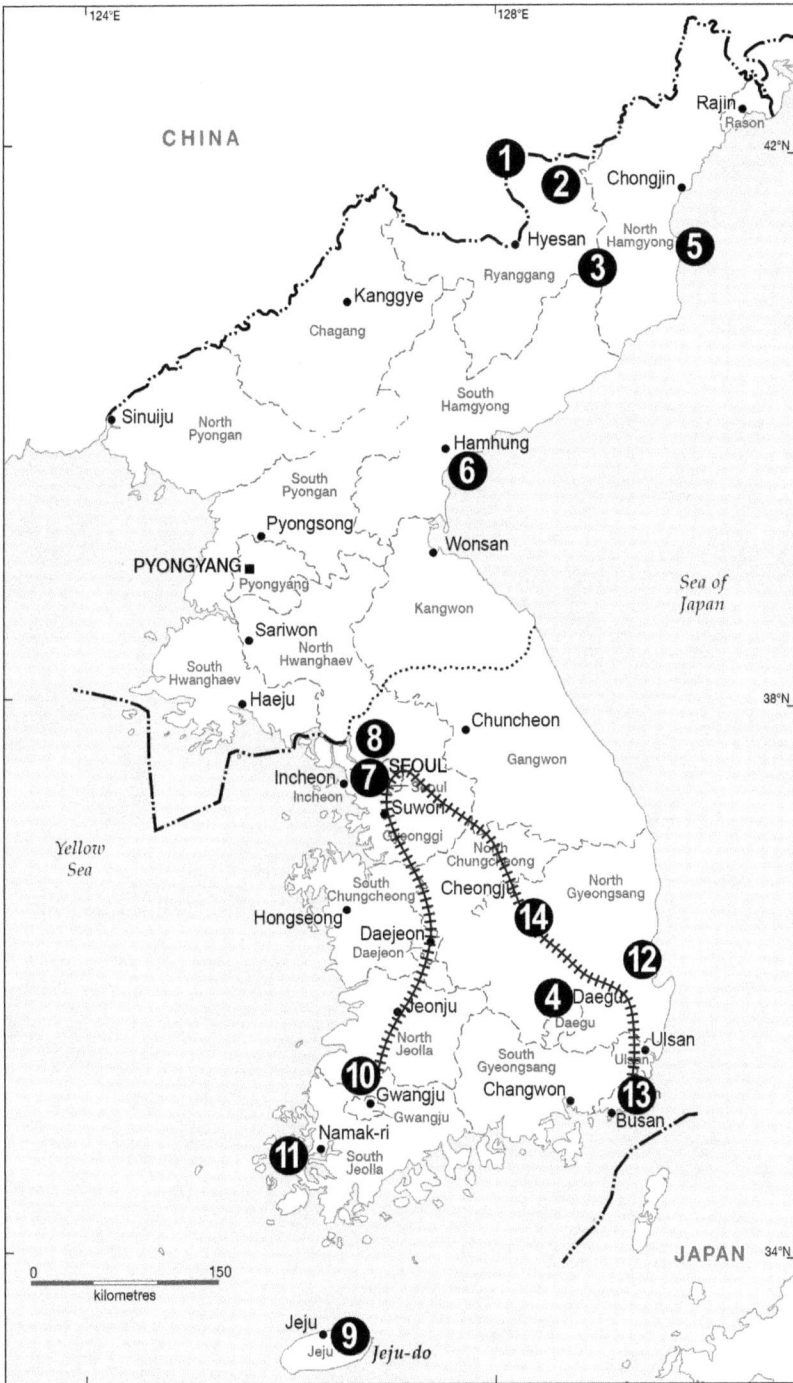

PROLOGUE - 1910
Chosen, The Land of the Broken Calm

The little story, "Yadool," is based on a lively, but minimal, understanding of the history of Korea. For centuries Korea was referred to as "Chosen," translated as "Land of the Morning Calm," because of the beauty of the peninsula. However, cultural and economic history of the Korean peninsula is one of intervention and influence of Chinese, Manchurian, Japanese, and Russian nations. The nationalization of Korea began with the period of the Three Kingdoms, Koguryo, Paekche and Silla, which lasted from 57 B.C.E. to 668 A.D. In these centuries the kingdoms, independent from one another, embraced a sense of community and common interests, far advanced from the early tribal affiliations. The Tang Dynasty in China was particularly influential in the Silla Kingdom and introduced agricultural production and government policies. Throughout the peninsula's history Chinese dynasties used military intervention, and affected economic and cultural progress. During these early centuries, Japanese pirates ravished the striving kingdoms and devastated struggling economies.

Vastly significant to the cultural evolution of the Korean peninsula was the introduction and spread of Buddhism. Originating in India, the worship of Buddha spread widely throughout China. Chinese Buddhist sects introduced the religion to Korea. Buddhist belief in a cycle of life, culminating in a paradise for those faithful to the doctrine, gave a sense of purpose and hope to early Koreans. Korean scholars studied in Chinese monasteries. In the Kingdom of Silla, Buddhism was associated with knighthood, which became translated into *Hwarang* warriors. These young men led a disciplined, Spartan life and developed the physical skills to protect others, which later lead to a systemized Martial Arts agenda.

In the tenth century the China's Tang Dynasty weakened, and a strong Korean general led a non-violent revolt, overthrew the Silla Kingdom, and established the Koryo Dynasty. The Koryo Dynasty began with a strong militant aspect in an effort to subdue outlying, isolated tribes. However, they maintained many of the Silla government procedures, as well as the Confucian pattern of administration. Two events dominated the Koryo period. Horse riding Mongolian warriors swept through the mountain passes, overran the peninsula, and routed the Koryo reign. The Mongols had widespread contacts with the Middle East, and even Europe. They ushered into Korea more cultural innovations, modified social structure, and introduced more social mobility within the Buddhist and military hierarchies. The Mongols fought with the Japanese pirates who continued to raid the peninsula. Kublai Khan invaded Japan on two occasions in the thirteenth century, using Korea as a military jumping off point.

A second, and more profound, impact on Korea was the introduction of Confucianism. Also imported from China by Korean scholars, this new religion emphasized order, righteousness, and propriety. Buddhism had degenerated into weakness and decadence, as well as an association with the Mongol invaders. As monks and abbots no longer provided moral and spiritual leadership for a weary and war torn population, Confucianism provided a viable alternative. The ideas of wisdom and personal commitment fostered by Confucianism, matched the freeing of society from the monastic stronghold, as well as the desire to rid the country of the Mongols. Confucianism was a substantial factor in the overthrow of the Koryo Dynasty. However, Buddhism, even confined to monasteries and out of political and economic realm, remains, to this day, tightly entrenched in the Korean culture.

In the late fourteenth century the Chinese Ming Dynasty banished the Mongols from China. Echoing early history, the Chinese Ming Dynasty provided assistance to General Yi Sonke to establish a new Dynasty in Korea, the Yi Dynasty The Yi Dynasty ruled Korea for the next five centuries. Confucianism was instated as national philosophy. Ming patterns of government, including legal precepts, were followed. Land reforms allowed the middle class and retired soldiers to settle in the pioneer northern part of the peninsula. A written language, and printing innovations, promised widespread literacy. Towns and villages were self sufficient, and the scholar class built many schools.

Troubles for the Yi Dynasty originated from outside nations. Korea's close ties with China made it vulnerable to the turmoil between China and Japan. Japan launched an invasion of China, through Korea. The fighting between these two nations lasted six years. By the time Chinese and Japanese forces finally withdrew, the progressive Yi Dynasty suffered economic devastation. Deep loathing of Japan emerged as Koreans watched the destruction of their towns and villages.

The withdrawal of foreign forces did not return peace and prosperity to the peninsula. The Manchus of Manchuria swept the Chinese Ming Dynasty from power. The Manchus quickly assimilated Chinese government and culture. Once established in China, the Manchus invaded Korea to punish Korean leaders and generals for loyally supporting the Ming Dynasty. Korea, again, was dominated by China, Manchu China.

During the eighteenth and nineteenth centuries, the concept of colonization was introduced by the large Western nations. Particularly, these nations wished to intercede and influence economic progress of Asian countries, using the euphemisms of "protectorate" and "sphere of interest". These euphemisms minimized the need for militaries, and direct conflict with competing powers. The newly modernized Meiji government of Japan sought to join these colonizing efforts. Particularly, the Japanese wanted to subdue and punish Korea.

After the turmoil during the Yi Dynasty, Korea attempted to withdraw from most associations with other nations. After many years of hermit like economy and trade, Korea lagged far behind other modern nations in economic stability and technological progress. Korea was in a weakened stage. Political upheaval resulted and the peasantry became increasingly alienated from the fractious royal houses. The nation was ill equipped to face the modern world.

Japan had become vitalized politically and militarily. Japanese officials were insulted by Korea's refusal to establish trade and diplomatic relations. They wanted to sever Korea from China and make the small country a protectorate of Japan. Japan prevailed against China in the Sino-Japanese War and forced China to sign the Treaty of Shimonseki in 1895, which ended Korea's relationship with the Chinese Quin Dynasty. In the guise of initiating reforms Japan replaced the Korean Foreign Ministers and Consuls with Japanese military unions.

Japan prevailed against Russia in the 1905 Russo-Japanese War, thereby eliminating Japan's last rival for influence in Korea. Two months later, the Japan-Korea Treaty made Korea a Japanese protectorate. Reforms were enacted, including the reduction of the Korean military from 20,000 to 1000.

In 1910, the Minister of War of Japan finalized Japanese complete control over Korea with the Korea-Japan Treaty of 1910. The Prime Minister of Korea and Terauchi Masatake, who became the first Japanese Governor General of Korea, signed the treaty. Japan would rule Korea until the end of World War II in 1945.

Korea became the largest Japanese settlement in the world. The Japanese settlers trampled upon all aspects of Korean culture. They corrupted Korean ethnic views. They assimilated into the Japanese culture those practices seen as acceptable. The Military Police were especially eager to ameliorate the influence and strength of Korean martial skills. Since the days of the Hwarang warriors, Korean martial arts have been integral to the peninsula's philosophical core. Martial skills were vital to survival of Korea as a nation and a culture. The growth of organized martial arts training centers accompanied and contributed to the growth of Korean nationalism. Now, literal extinction threatened them.

The following story begins a few years after the 1910 complete subjugation of Korea. The small village of Sinuju lies on the slopes of Mt Paektu, on the northern border of Korea, directly below China. In fact, the northern slopes of the mountain are part of China. Taekeon Master Kija leads a small band of martial artists in Sinuju. Master Kija and his young troops are faced with a momentous task; they must save the Taeguek Circle.

MASTER KIJA

The old man climbed slowly; his head bent; his arms clasped in front of him. His sandaled foot brushed against the damp mountainside and a dislodged stone cracked against the rocks, popped into the air, and disappeared into the mist, far below. He continued, impervious to the muffled echoes of the falling rock. The cold April wind howled and tore at his clothing as he pushed up the stony ledge. He struggled up the steep slopes and volcanic rubble of Mount Paektu, his breath ragged and thunderous in his ears.

Mount Paektu reigns as the highest and grandest of all of Korea's mountains. Master Kija, like most Koreans, believed Mt. Paektu to be sacred, the spiritual birthplace of their culture. Sixteen peaks surround the crater in which lies Heaven Lake, the source of the Songhua, Tumen, and Yalu rivers. A two hundred thirty foot waterfall spills majestically from the lake and shrouds the lower slopes with haze. On Mount Paektu, the godly Tan-gun founded the Kingdom of Chosen, and the beginning of the Korean nation, thousands of years ago. Master Kija labored up the sacred mountain with a present, timely desperation. Deep within its volcanic bowels was hidden a secret, the spiritual source of survival for Korea. Three other Korean *Tae Keon* Masters knew of this crucial secret. Master Kija guarded it.

At last, the old man ascended through the last wisps of clouds. Brilliant sunlight assaulted him. He stopped and flung his head up. His hooded eyes widened and he exhaled explosively. "Oh, Divine one, give me the strength I need!" Master Kija realized he had spoken aloud and a sudden awareness swept throughout him. He straightened and focused his attention beyond the narrow, treacherous ledge beneath his feet. Mists spiraled below him as if a live presence were revealing and then concealing craggy mountaintops. Those peaks evoked giant steppingstones amidst a blanket of snow. The old man envisioned the quiet beauty of the valleys and slopes that skirted the various peaks. "Chosen, land of the morning calm," he thought, this time silently. "But, no!" he choked. "It is the land of a broken calm."

He leaned into the cold air, swung his arms, and willed the rest of his tired body forward. He was anxious to reach his cave before his students did. The trail widened and he carefully maneuvered over sharp edged boulders, debris from centuries of eruptions. The last eruption occurred a mere seven years ago, and spewed one more layer of ashen rock upon the eons of residue, creating the illusion of an impassable barrier to ascension by mere humans. Master Kija believed the formidable appearance of the tumbled mountain provided a great measure of safety for his small troop of martial artists.

"Since the great age of the Chosen Empire, hundreds

of years ago, Chinese, Russian, and Japanese forces have been fighting over, and dividing Korea into territorial chunks." He reminisced. He was acutely aware of the contentious history of his beloved land. Master Kija could not fathom that one nation would ultimately dominate the entire peninsula. In fact, he secretly believed, but would never admit, that the constant, disruptions of foreigners had one positive aspect. Mount Paektu would continue to harbor, unhindered, Korea's greatest secret. The Sacred Circle, the *Taegeuk*, would remain safe from discovery. The never-ending hostilities left no one enemy nation the freedom to search throughout the unfriendly, mountainous terrain.

Master Kija was shocked when Japan defeated the powerful Russian Empire in 1905. Japan's entry spelled disaster for Korea. Now, the Japanese Emperor was unimpeded in his desire to completely subjugate the Koreans. There were, already, thousands of Japanese immigrants on the peninsula. Thus it was a simple step when Japan annexed Korea with the Japan-Korea Treaty of 1910. This treaty, signed by Korean Prime Minister Lee Wan-yung, made Terauchi Masatake the first Japanese Governor General of Korea.

In order to quell any disturbances or revolts by the Koreans, the Imperial Army put the Military Police in control. Master Kija was afraid the police would control the Korean peninsula for many more years. This was the period that Master Kija and other *Tae Keon* Masters dreaded most of all. The Police had the authority to control the country in every way. Chosen was not broken. Chosen was lost.

Again, he stumbled, and a small rush of rocks splayed against the granite wall and rocketed beyond the ledge. He muttered and shook his head in despair. "They brutalize us! They corrupt our martial skills and drive us into the caves. My arrogance kept me from taking action!" A thunderous realization struck him, weakened his knees, and drove him down to the ledge.

"The Japanese Emperor has been told of our treasure! The Japanese ruling families always believed the ancient lore about the mysterious *Taegeuk*, and the power of 'the Yadool'. He may not know the exact form of the treasure, as it is, simultaneously, spiritual, mythical, and capable of tremendous power. The Emperor's mercenaries and spies have been searching for the *Taeguek* for decades. Why would they suddenly suspect that our sacred mountain holds the secret? Only four living Masters of *Tae Keon*, including myself, understand the immensity of the secret, and the peril involved. Have they captured one of them? I must contact the other Masters immediately."

His steps faltered slightly as he thought about the immediate danger. "That must be why the soldiers invaded our little village. Mt. Paektu lies in the Chanbaek Mountain range in the northern extremity, next to China." Master Kija pondered. "Only the Major and his soldiers have been ordered to this northern outpost of Sinuju. Almost the entire military occupation of thousands is congregated towards Seoul. This must be the reason that Major Yamagata and his Japanese soldiers stormed into our village. This must be why the soldiers have crammed into our small homes and confiscated everything, even our food. The Major must be waiting further instructions from Imperial Japan."

Master Kija was severely angry with himself. He underestimated the total penetration of an enemy occupation. He did not foresee the violence, and the cold-blooded acts of cruelty. His anger propelled him up a particularly steep ledge.

"These poor people," he thought. "The Major's men tossed the villagers from their homes and his Japanese soldiers moved in. Whole families have to live in the cold, muddy streets, and they do not know why. The Japanese military make the men and women labor without food, and they do not know why they are being treated so brutally. Koreans are starving to death and dying in their own fields, and they do not know why!"

"I am devastated! My blindness is unforgiveable!" Master Kija berated himself. For many years, he opened hearts and minds of young boys to the martial arts of *Tae Keon*. He believed the tenets and discipline practiced in his small dojang brought meaning and hope to the children. When the soldiers occupied their village, Master Kija's little troop was forced to practice their forms in shadows. As more and more Japanese soldiers jammed into Sinuju, they fled the village. Master Kija set up a dojang in a clearing in the foothills of Mt. Paektu. The cold weather dispelled hopes of remaining in the clearing. Finally, he moved the dojang into the safest place, a large cavern among a chain of caves, deep in the heart of the volcano. The students loved the primitive grandeur of the high, craggy walls. They happily shared their meals and practiced their forms on the hard ground. Young faces glowed in the flickering flame of the large fire they tended. Shadows on the cave walls echoed each kick and leap. He relished the safety and comfort of the cave.

Now, however, searching soldiers, with bayonets fixed, banished any hope of safety and comfort. The danger was real, tangible, and close. His bony face contorted, he anguished aloud. "Oh why did I not take steps sooner?" He lurched dangerously close to the edge of misty nothingness. "I was so smug, so complacent in my small world! I should have acted much sooner."

His deepest fear, his cruelest nightmare, spurred Master Kija's pace. He edged around the seemingly impassable wall of boulders and entered the massive cave that served as his dojang. He faced the cave wall on which hung the *Hwarang* code of values, principles of conduct for his students. His students often made the arduous trek up the mountainside. Now, they must dodge Japanese soldiers and cross the lower slopes in darkness. "Perhaps I still have some time, before the students arrive."

Master Kija walked, unsteadily, through a dark corridor of rock. A beam of sunlight rayed down from an open crevice to the sky. Here, he kept his pigeons in sturdy bamboo cages. He dipped into a barrel of seed and sprinkled seed into the trough. He reached for a square of parchment from a neat stack in a cleft in the wall.

A soft sound caused Master Kija to turn and look back through the tunnel. Eui sook Chung had entered the dojang. He groaned inwardly, quickly returned the parchment, and walked back into the light of the cave. Eui sook was his youngest student, and a girl. The boys reluctantly accepted this newest student because she could outrun all of them except for Hyan Cho. She dressed like them in wide baggy trousers, tied at the ankle, and topped with a short jacket. Her pocketed vest was a vibrant blue instead of the drab grey and brown vests worn by the boys.

Many months ago, Master Kija found the little girl dirty, famished, and hiding in thickets. He brought her to the cave and coaxed her story from her. Her mother and newborn brother were convalescing when the soldiers arrived and demanded residence. Eui sook's father resisted. Major Yamagata's soldiers shot and killed all but Eui sook, who fled to her grandparents in the next village. Her broken-hearted grandparents did not want a living reminder of their loss. Eui sook fled again. Master Kija persuaded Chul Moo, his oldest student, to let Eui sook join his small commune of orphans in Sinuju.

Master Kija was not quite sure how she would handle the task he was about to introduce. Her character had yet to be tested. She had become a chatterbox, so Kija put a finger to his lips, motioning her to be silent. Eui sook was so excited she overlooked his gesture. "Master, I had to hide in the creek and go around the entire village, for the barbarians are going house to house in search of, oh, I don't know!" Eui sook's long braids danced around her head. She knew no fear in the safety of the *dojang*. "They speed through the streets in their funny looking vehicles and do not care who they run over! The soldiers found that some of the older boys joined the guerillas in the forests. They bound their relatives and beat them with hard sticks. No one dared to interfere, because the other soldiers sat on the lorries and pointed their guns at us." She stopped abruptly and plopped down to the grass mat. "I don't feel well. Perhaps I ran too fast on that last mile."

Once Eui sook quieted on the mat, Master Kija quickly slipped back into the corridor where he kept his pigeons. He released a latch on one of the bamboo cages. The small pigeon sprang atop the cage and fluttered his silky feathers. Master Kija hurriedly wrote his message. He affixed the parchment to the pigeon's leg and raised his palm upwards. The little bird rose into the air, spiraled slowly to the sunlit crevice, and disappeared.

In the following hours, the six boys followed Eui sook Chung into the cave, one by one. Each collapsed onto the grass rushes and gasped for breath. Sounds of their harsh breathing echoed throughout the cave. Wide, dark eyes followed Master Kija as he paced silently before them. Each student was wildly curious about the Master's summons. The danger was great now that armed Japanese soldiers roamed Sinuju and the surrounding fields and forests. Still, Master Kija insisted that they make the long travail up the mountain, in broad daylight!

The two older boys carried large jars of kimchi. They placed the jars against the stone, and began a coal fire in the pit, which would gradually warm some of the cave, and become hot enough to warm the kimchi.

Master Kija apprised each of them. All the children were extremely thin. Still, they did not look malnourished, as many of the villagers in Sinuju looked. Small muscle formations defined their skinny arms and legs, and each child sat or stood tall. Jung sup Kim was the oldest at 14 years, and the gravest. He was, possibly, the most skilled in martial arts among his fellow students. Jung sup Kim obsessively researched every topic that arose in the dojangs. Often, Master Kija hastened to review his own research so that he may be accurate in his responses. He viewed Jung sup Kim with some promise.

Hyun Cho, twelve years old, was the strongest and fastest. The other students could dare Hyun Cho to do anything, and Master Kija often had to temper their imaginative challenges. Hyun Cho liked to stay in the cavernous dojang long after the others left. He swept the slate floor, cleaned the pigeon cages, and refilled the water jugs. All the while humming contently under his breath.

Chin Ho's dry wit and quick thought brought levity and amusement into the dojang. His tall, lean body lent the impression of greater age than his twelve years. His black eyes flashed with secret merriment, which might burst forth at any moment. Master Kija sensed, and relied on, a depth of intellect behind Chin Ho's droll, and sometimes sarcastic, rejoinders.

Extremely skinny and short, Chang nom Kim wore round rimless spectacles, which magnified his large brown eyes to alien proportions. He seldom spoke and kept to himself as much as possible. The Japanese soldiers shot his father and his older brother fled to the forest, presumably in search of guerilla bands. He and his mother scavenged for food. The others knew about his family and did not resent his aloofness. Master Kija thought it difficult to know the mind of this frail eleven year old. When not performing his *poomse*, the boy was silent and still, except for excessively pushing his ugly glasses back into place.

Fidgety Hee yung Kim was almost as irrepressible as Eui sook. Unlike the other boys who kept their hair cropped close to their scalps, Hee yung Kim had a wild mop of black hair that seemed to thrash about, independently. Master Kija thought he couldn't sit still for a haircut. His scrawny body constantly moved. Even sitting, his feet would move up and down. "Hee yung Kim, focus!" I must say these words a hundred times a session, Master Kija thought to himself. He worried that Hee yung Kim, like little Eui sook, would not be up to the chilling task ahead.

At thirteen years old, Chul Moo has been with me the longest, Master Kija mused. He, too, seldom spoke. He usually tried to tuck his large, awkward body into the smallest dimension. Master Kija's continual challenge was to get Chul Moo to lengthen his stances, embrace his tallness. The other students believed Chul Moo to be a little slow. Master Kija appreciated their tolerance and acceptance of Chul Moo, even as he, himself, was not quite sure of his mental acuity. Perhaps he was too fond of him to make a harsh judgment. The boys sprawled close together. Eui sook Chung sat a little apart from them.

"Listen carefully," he finally began, "for we are now facing a great danger, a threat even greater than loss of our lives!" The children looked at each other, then, focused again on the Master. Master Kija cleared this throat. He wondered how to begin his narrative. How could he make the children understand the urgency? He decided to plunge into the story. Their questions would help him fill in the long tale.

MASTER KIJA SPEAKS

"Korea's greatest treasure, the 'Sacred Circle,' the eight *Taegeuks* and the origins of our art and survival, is hidden deep in these caverns. The 'Circle' has been hidden here for centuries. Should the enemy discover this treasure, they would storm this mountain, and perhaps kill us all. The very existence of Korean culture is severely threatened."

"Waaah!" Eui sook clamped her hand over her mouth, ashamed at her involuntary wail. Jung sup Kim drew in his breath with a sharp hiss. The other boys straightened to sitting position with shocked expressions.

"Is that why Major Yamagata and all his soldiers have invaded Sinuju?" Of course, Jung sup Kim would recognize the immediate problem.

"I've made a mistake! Proceed slowly," Master Kija reprimanded himself. He drew a deep uneasy breath, and continued.

"Yes, I have finally faced that fact." He responded to

Jung sup Kim. "However, there is so much more you should know. So much more! Please be patient, while I explain why the danger is so great. I must start at the beginning."

But Master Kija stood still and silent for many minutes. The students were used to his stillness. However, after a few minutes Hee yung Kim jumped up and shuffled his feet back and forth. Tears filled Eui sook's wide eyes and ran down her chin. Jung sup Kim, Hyun Cho, Chin Ho and Chang nom Kim all began to stir, impatiently. Chul Moo sat motionless, his eyes fixed on Master Kija.

Finally, the Master raised both hands outward and slowly brought them down. With this motion Hee yung Kim sank to his knees, and all movement stopped among the others. He began. "I have told you at one time of the legend of the eight *kwaes*. The *kwae* represents the universal symbol of the *yin/yang*, the immortal principle from which life springs: the manner in which we the people experience the universe."

"But Master," Hyun Cho interrupted. "The story of the *kwaes* is ancient history, mythical even. How can this myth be relevant to what the Japanese are doing to our village?" Eui sook choked off her gasp with both hands. Chul Moo seemed to shrink against the wall. The other boys froze in place. Hyun Cho not only spoke without permission, he argued with the Master!

Now, Master Kija simply stood before them again, still as stone. His eyes were black and trained far beyond the cave in which they gathered. He seemed almost to be in a trance. They were used to his silences, accepting these phases as a part of his normally taciturn demeanor. He straightened, focused his eyes, and continued as if Hyun Cho had not rudely interrupted him.

"There is a much deeper meaning to the *kwaes*, and the *Taegeuk* that symbolize them, than you have yet to understand." Master Kija frowned and wrinkled his brow. His voice rose. "We know that the core of *Tae Keon* philosophy is rooted in Buddhist history. You must understand how important this history is to us and to the treasure that we protect. Ancient Buddhism views the universe as a dynamic entity that constantly changes. The *Taegeuk* circle echoes this philosophy. The *Taegeuk* circle, also called the *Ying/Yang*, is composed of eight opposing forces, or *kwaes*, that represent the cyclical flow of the universe. The *Taegeuk* forms, which you have studied and performed, are the literal interpretation of each of these eight forces."

"What treasure?" asked Hyun Cho.

"The 'Sacred Circle of the *Ying/Yang*' ignorant one," Jung sup Kim answered. He continued, "Master, we have been studying the eight *Taegeuk* forms and we know of their importance to our martial arts training."

"*Kmoen*", Master Kija spoke in agitation. 'Let me finish!" Jung sup Kim quickly looked at his feet. Although shamed, he was also surprised. Master Kija never barked at his students. His silence, alone, kept them in line. Now, his entire body seemed to vibrate, and his voice was harsh.

Master Kija continued, "You have experienced each *Taegeuk* as a martial art and do not fully realize the power within the entire form. Each block, strike or kick is vital to a one's defense. There is so much more to each pattern of blocks and strikes. A *Taegeuk*, ably performed, can bequeath the knowledge and strength necessary to save you! Knowledge of your *Taegeuk* will allow each of you to have the ultimate power of preservation." He waved his hands dramatically, an effect not usually in his manner.

Again, the students looked at one another in disbelief. "Save us?"

Chul Moo thought to himself with a deep sense of foreboding. "Master Kija is raising his voice and waving his hands! What kind of catastrophe would arouse that behavior? What must we do?" He looked at his fellow students. Each of them had stiffened; seven pairs of eyes staring, fixedly, at their Master.

"I have neglected to deepen your knowledge. No! You are so young! We would have come to that stage of your understanding. Now, however, time is precious, and we must jump years ahead in your training". Master Kija realized that his agitated manner was a distraction to his message. He took a calming breath. "You only know the movements. You do not yet know the ancient wisdom, the spiritual message intrinsic in each of the movements. You do not yet understand the power of the eight *kwae* when united into the original sacred form.

Hee yung Kim squirmed a bit. Jung sup Kim poked him with his elbow and hissed, "Be still!"

Master Kija looked down upon their anxious faces and realized he must slow down and use less scary rhetoric. "I will back up and talk about what they already know," he mused, silently. His students knew the physical moves of the *Taegeuk* forms they faithfully practiced, even as each was at a different stage in their progression.

Master Kija began with the basics and reminded the children that each *poomse* is essential to the achievement of powerful fighting skills. He talked about the three level progression of each poomse. He was confident each student had mastered the first level, knowledge of their individual *Taegeuk*, for they practiced diligently. Jung sup Kim, Hyun Cho, and Chin Ho, he thought, could envision an opponent in each move. "Now you must understand the third, and most important, level!" He sharply looked from one student to another. "You must breathe life into the form. You must become the form!"

Worried dark eyes flicked back and forth. Eui sook jumped up, plopped down, and stood up again, uncharacteristically silent. Master Kija continued. "I cannot teach you how this level is accomplished. It is within each of you to arrive at this consciousness, to breathe the power of the *Taegeuk*. It is imperative that you become the weapon intrinsic in the form. Only when you attain the spiritual essence of the *Taegeuk* will you reach a measure of safety."

"I thought we were finally safe in this cave." Chin Ho raised his hand, but spoke before Master Kija assented. "I don't think the foreigners even know about our trail, or that there are any caves up here. They've been searching for months."

"No, no," the old man flung his arms out. "I don't mean we are in immediate danger. Danger is coming. The Major's men realize there is some guerilla activity in the forests around our mountain. They are searching everyone's home and fields. I do not think the soldiers will attempt to climb our mountain until they have finished searching in the villages. A darker peril threatens us."

Just as Master Kija realized that he must get to the point, Chin Ho spoke out again. "Master, your message said we must hurry. I felt it was urgent, like an emergency." The others nodded. Yes, they each thought there was an emergency.

"It is urgent!" He gestured out in frustration. "But it is not the kind of emergency that is easily dealt with." He forced himself to calm down. They were children! He must impress upon them magnitude of the situation, without paralyzing them with fear. That would certainly put them in great jeopardy. "Let me continue," He said, "and you will understand why you were summoned from your homes in such a way."

"May we sit?" Chin Ho dared to ask. At some point, they had stood up and positioned themselves in front of the Master, as if beginning class. Master Kija's head moved a fraction higher. Each student fell gratefully into a sitting crossed leg position.

"I will finish telling you why we are gathered this morning. We must act quickly for events are moving at a faster pace than thought." Master Kija knew he was repeating himself as he searched for the right words.

GRANDMASTER JUN CHUL:
THE VISION AND THE PLAN

"There is a reason why it is vital for you to have intensive knowledge of the *Taegeuks*. I am asking each of you to embark upon an extremely dangerous mission. I know you have courage and strength. Your mission is so dangerous; you will need a greater means of defense. I repeat. When you understand the essence of the *Taegeuk* spirit, you will be able to use the power necessary to survive. You will not be helpless against the jeopardy that is outside this cave."

They did not move and none of them dared to ask, "what dangerous mission?"

Master Kija recited a brief history of the facts behind Japan's conquest. At first, the scholarly Jung sup Kim leaned his chin on his hand and listened to each word in rapt attention. The old Master began telling of the tremendous tragedies and hardships suffered by Koreans through the ages. Koreans faced virtual starvation and no hope of anything other than a future filled with continued devastation. He did not go into the details of wars, treaties and betrayals. He portrayed a vivid picture of victimization and misery, barely mitigated by the spirit of Buddhism, or the reason of Confucianism. Stirred by his reach into the past, the Master's face became flushed and his voice rose dramatically.

Jung sup Kim jerked up and his hand fell into his lap. Master Kija paused, and looked at each young face as comprehension touched upon it. Their immediate plight in Sinuju had, thus far, seemed a harsh game; one in which each of them saw vengeance and reward when the game was beat. Now, one by one, the students began to see the invasion of their village as a continuation of a sad history; a history of inexorable tragedy.

"I cannot bear this," Master Kija thought to himself. " I have taken away the last vestiges of innocence. I have stolen their hope and enthusiasm and replaced it with hopelessness and sorrow." When he looked at Eui sook, sitting apart from the boys, he saw the tears he knew he would see.

"I have to go on," he whispered to himself. He continued his recitation with a heavy heart and a resolute soul.

"Now, I will tell you about the ordeal that faces us. I will begin with a story of a vision." In a hushed, reverent voice, Master Kija began with the vision on Mt. Paektu. "Years ago, after the First Sino-Japanese War, and Korea granted independence, some *Tae Keon* Masters did not believe the bloodshed was truly over. Grandmaster Jun Chul climbed high on this sacred mountain and began a long meditation. A vision came to him."

"I've never heard of Grandmaster Jun Chul," interrupted Chul Moo, "and his name is like mine." All of them were surprised at Chul Moo's outburst. Chin Ho rolled his eyes. Chul Moo rarely spoke out and his fellow students suspected that Chul Moo truly did not understand everything said. Instinctively, Chin Ho kept these thoughts about Chul Moo to himself.

"Grandmaster Jun Chul practiced *Tae Keon* many years in the Doseonsa Temple, in the foothills of Mount Samgaksan. He no longer taught young people. Masters of *Tae Keon* sought his wisdom and enjoyed the solace of his presence. I was his student when he and I were both younger." The Master could see, by their expressions, they could not imagine him as a mere student. "The Grandmaster was old then and has since died. He left us a great vision; revelations that may help us save the *kwaes*."

Master Kija continued. "During Grandmaster's meditation the great philosopher, Sinsi Bonski, appeared before him. In the ancient year, 35 B.C.E, the heavenly spirits commanded philosopher Bonski to observe the universal truths and rituals of heaven. The philosopher comprised eight divinations from his observations, and he passed them down to our people. We received each of the eight divinations in the form of a sacred *kwae*."

"In final form, there are eight *kwaes* placed on the outer circumference of the *Taegeuk* circle, also known as the *yin/yang*. The *yin/yang* is represented inside the circle. Each *kwae* is physically interpreted in a *Taegeuk* form. Each of you is practicing one of the *Taegeuk poomses*. As you practice and attain the ultimate knowledge of the *Taegeuk poomse*, you will realize the meaning and spirit of the *kwae*. In our *dojang* we call the eight Taegeuks by the name of the eighth, *Yadool*."

"In this vision, philosopher Bonski beseeched the Grandmaster to save the divine *Taegeuk*. He warned that Korea would face terrible suffering under a foreign invader. The philosopher even informed Grandmaster Jun Chul that the barbarians would try to find and capture the *Taegeuk*. The enemy would use the power of the *Taegeuk* for evil purposes and impel Diaspora upon *Tae Keon* spirit."

MEANING OF THE EIGHT TAEGEUKS

IL-JANG
KEON
HEAVEN

O-JANG
SEON
WIND

Yi-JANG
TAE
LAKE

SAM-JANG
RA
FIRE

Yuk-JANG
KAM
WATER

Chil-JANG
KAN
MOUNTAIN

Sa-JANG
JIN
THUNDER

Pol-JANG
GAN
EARTH

REPRESENTAVE KWAES

"Grandmaster Jun Chul suspected that the Imperial family of Japan knew about the sacred *Taegeuk*. He also realized that eventually Korea would be overrun and occupied by the Japanese, who had already defeated the strong bear of Russia. The prophecy haunted the Grandmaster. He knew he must take steps to carry out Philosopher Bonki's quest. He sent away three messengers to summon *Tae Keon* Masters from temples and *dojangs* in Korea. The messengers traveled as far south as the island of Jeju, and nearer to us on the Tumen River, which is directly under the Chinese nation. I was already in Sinuju, and believed we could gather in the village. We were all surprised when the Grandmaster led us deep in the caverns of Mt. Paektu."

"Once we were all gathered, Grandmaster Jun Chul revealed the vision. We were stricken, aghast. No one word could describe our fear. Naturally, we accepted the truth of the vision. We had already experienced Philosopher Bonki's prophecy through our history, when one nation or another overran our peninsula. And now Korea was intensely populated by the Japanese. We were, for all intents and purposes, practically a colony of Japan. The Grandmaster was right to assemble us in this secret place. All four of us felt the burden and responsibility that Grandmaster Jun Chul, alone, had carried."

"The Grandmaster led us in meditation. Our mission was to formulate a way to protect our treasure, and our sacred heritage. After many days of meditation and contemplation, we conceived an outrageous plan! We were, at once, tremendously apprehensive and resolute."

"I, humbly, take credit for the original idea, for I remembered the Chataigne Service and the bold actions of the Abbess, Alouette Descoteaux, during the eighteenth century French Revolution. It took hours to explain how the Abbess saved the secret of the Chataigne Service. It took many more hours of persuasion before the other Masters would envision how we could use the same method to save the *Taegeuk*. Finally the other masters agreed with my idea, extreme as it was. We all knew that it was necessary to take drastic steps. Our plan to save the *Taegeuk* circle was this. We must tear the *Taegeuk* apart! With great apprehension, we separated each of the eight *kwaes* from the Taegeuk circle. Oh, we were fearful! Once divided, the *Taegeuk*, the Sacred Circle, lost its universal spirit, and its venerable power."

Master Kija did not notice the tears running down his furrowed cheeks. The students did. Appearance of the Master's tears stunned them as nothing else could. He continued. "Once we separated the *kwaes*, we knew we had to disperse each to a destination, far away from each other. The greatest power lies in the unity of the entire *Taegeuk* circle, all eight *kwaes*. The Japanese could, conceivably discover one *kwae*, or even two or three *kwaes*, and wrest them from the hiding places. The supremacy of the *Taegeuk* circle would still elude them. Remember, the spiritual force of the *Taegeuk* only occurs in the presence of the united eight!"

Jung sup Kim noticed that the Master was repeating himself, and wondered if the others noticed.

Master Kija sensed that only the Jung sup Kim and

Chin Ho were accurately following his story. He determinedly continued. "We knew we had to hide the *kwaes* far away from each other. Our plan, then, was to transport the *kwaes* from the protection of the cave, and deliver them safely to their destinations on the Korean peninsula. As an additional precaution, we went to great lengths to disguise each of them. We placed each of the eight *kwaes* into statuary of pure gold. Jewels encrusted the statues, so each appeared to be some kind of pagan religious idol. A code, outlined by the jewels, depicted the contents of the statue."

"Then, we realized we had a further problem. We trapped ourselves as we gathered here in this cave. Once we had completed our work, we had no means by which to disperse the idols. Korea would soon be subject to Japanese martial law."

Master nodded at the students. "We were right to suspect that event. Now, even our small village of Sinuju is under the martial law of Major Yamagata. Also, the Japanese were inherently suspicious of our martial arts, and closely followed our activities. They would certainly notice five Masters of *Tae Keon* descending the mountain, even stealthily, and in darkness. Fortunately, they did not know about the cave. They were too busy with farming and such to consider climbing a difficult, probably impassable, mountain path. However, we could not take such a chance. We could not draw any attention to the source of the trail, or our mountain. We had not thought this when we gathered to make this decision, as we did not know we would each have one or two idols among our persons."

Now, intently, his students followed the Master's words. "We had to keep the idols here, in this cavern, until we found some way to spirit them out. Each idol, or statuary, is hidden within the walls of this cave." Hee yung Kim swiveled around, as if he could spot one of the secret hiding places. Jung sup Kim jabbed him with his elbow again.

"Many years have passed since the statuary was hidden in these caves. We will have to seek each one from its hidden location." Master Kija frowned at Hee Yung Kim. "Before he died, Grandmaster Jun Chul entrusted me, as the heavens commanded philosopher Bonki, to ensure that the enemy never attain the united *Taegeuk*. My mission in life, heretofore, has been to teach discipline and philosophy. My greater mission, I reveal to you now, is to protect this treasure. I alone know the location of each of the *Taegeuk*." He was repeating himself again. Jung sup Kim supposed the Master was under great stress.

THE TWO OPTIONS

Master Kija paused, and drew another deep breath. "I have two options. The first option, and perhaps the most difficult choice, is this. We can locate each of these statuaries, and destroy them. Then they would never fall into the hands of our enemy."

Jung sup Kim gasped and jumped to his feet. "You said your mission is to protect the treasure!"

Eui sook also jumped to her feet. That she sat long as she did was a miracle. She shook her finger at Jung sup Kim. "You didn't address Master Kija."

Master Kija nodded his head, glad about their attention to his story. "I rejected that path!" he declared. "The great power and wisdom within the *Taegeuk* circle is sacred. Even had we time to destroy these pieces or to deface them beyond recognition, I still would not choose that path. The power inherent in the *Taegeuk* circle will be exploited as an instrument for the good of humankind, not destroyed.

The students nodded in unison. Master Kija continued with a degree of satisfaction. "The second option is to recover each of the statuary and then scatter the eight *kwaes* far apart: a solution we Masters agreed to years ago. This is the most reasonable option; a path proved successful by the courageous Abbess, Alouette Descoteaux."

"Who is this Abbess, Alouette Descoteaux?" Eui sook asked.

"What?" Master Kija turned towards Eui sook, still sitting apart from the boys. "Oh, well, Eui sook, I will tell you later."

"By scattering the statues far from each other, it is likely that the Japanese would be unable to recover all the idols. The enemy must never have access to '*Yadool*'. They must not steal its power from Korea. I believe our solution of separation and wide dispersion is the best, maybe the only way to protect 'the eight'. Perhaps one day, if history permits, we can recover the sacred eight for the greater good of the universe."

They were all standing now. Chin Ho asked "but what if the Japanese catch us with the idols?"

"The Japanese are not likely to be suspicious if a child is walking a road," Replied Master Kija. "You will slip off the mountain and to your destinations separately, and at different times."

THE ABBESS,
ALOUETTE DESCOTEAUX

"Master", Hyun Cho asked, "Why is the quantity of eight so important"?

Master Kija thought in silence for many minutes. Then he began. "I am not fully competent about the significance or the sacredness of the number eight. I do know that the number 'eight' contains a spiritual, mythical quality many times in the history of the world." Master Kija arranged his robes and sat down in front of his little class. We Masters of *Tae Keon* are impressed with the most recent historical episode involving the number eight. It also is the story of a courageous Abbess, Alouette Descoteaux. This mystery surrounds the Emperor Charlemagne, and the Chataigne Service."

"I remember studying about Charlemagne!" exclaimed Jung sup Kim. "He was King of the Franks and the first Holy Roman Emperor. He ruled hundreds of years, and he was a great warrior!"

"Yes he was," Master Kija replied, with a small smile. "But, Charlemagne ruled over most of Europe for forty-seven years. Men only lived hundreds of years in the Protestant Bible. This story of eight begins when Caliph Harun al Rashid, Moslem governor of Barcelona, presented Emperor Charlemagne with a beautiful chess set, complete with a stunning silver and gold board. The Emperor did not know the game of chess; only that the Caliph's gift was a set of the most wondrous carvings he had ever seen. The Emperor set his gift aside, as a treasure to behold."

Master Kija told his students that upon Charlemagne's fortieth birthday celebration, he invited a young man, Galwain the Frank, to play a game of chess on this service. Galwain won the match, for he knew how to play the game. During the game, hallucinations and rages seized both men in turn. Charlemagne feared the set was evil, as he nearly killed Galwain in a fit during the match. Other stories of bloodshed and violence surrounded the service. The Emperor and Galwain conspired to bury the chess service within the walls of Galwain's Chataigne Fortress, deep in the French Pyrenees. Charlemagne placed a curse on the set and vowed it never be extracted from the fortress. When Galwain de Chataigne lay ill and dying years later, he bequeathed the territory of Chataigne to the Church. He also told the story of the Emperor's curse, inscribed above the Abbey entrance. The Church, habitually fearful of evil powers, agreed to not free the enigmatic chess set, now known as the Chataigne Service, from the massive walls of stone.

More than a thousand years later, Alouette Descoteaux, the current Abbess, knew, as all those before her knew, of the secret Chataigne Service hidden within the walls of the Chataigne Abbey. She felt the Abbey was relatively secure, tucked away in the French Pyrenees, many days distant from eighteenth century quagmire of uprisings and revolutions. The Abbess, and her eight charges, prayed and worked in quiet and contentment from dawn to dusk. They had little premonition of their imminent troubles.

The Reverend Mother felt she should share the secret of the Chataigne Service with another person, a person of some strength and power. She revealed the secret of the Chataigne Service to her childhood friend, Catherine the Great of Russia. Later, she felt she betrayed the trust given to her. However, the revelation to her friend saved her life, the lives of the nuns and novices of the Abbey, as well as the Chataigne treasure.

When Catherine was young, a mathematician and philosopher, aware of Catherine's impending greatness, warned her of a secret society of men, known as the Brotherhood of Freemasons. These men, he explained, claimed to know the mysteries of the ancients. They were the spiritual descendants of the men whose forbidden knowledge Caliph al-Rashid had encoded into the Chataigne Service. Catherine remembered these warnings.

Empress Catherine knew that Freemasons, to a great degree, fueled the flames of the French Revolution. Divergent classes of men including the educated bourgeoisie, the clergy, and the army shared certain beliefs and ideals, but believed they were blocked from social and political advancement. A separate contingent within the secret society, largely aristocrats and intellectuals, sought a deeper, more sinister result to the revolution they helped foster. These powerful men desired the power contained within the Chataigne Service. By evoking the powers of the chess set, the Empress knew, these men would not hesitate to topple monarchies into the dust and seize control of the world. Only two people knew of the actual existence of the Chataigne Service. Catherine the Great sent a trusted aide to the Abbey with an urgent message.

The Abbess gathered the six nuns and two young novices to her study. She told them the story of the Chataigne Service, and the danger they were in. It was their mission, she said, to remove the tool of evil and scatter it as far, and wide as possible

Master Kija stopped abruptly and frowned down at the children. "The Abbess understood that powerful men sought the evil potency within the Chataigne Service. She knew that her greatest calling was protection of the Service. This wise old woman willingly placed her loyal, pious, nuns at risk.

She recently received two young sisters from the Basque region of Spain as novices, Lukene and Geshima Velasco. The Abbess renamed the sisters, who were fair and green eyed, Cecile and Genevieve Chastain. As they were bilingual in both French and Spanish, the Abbess thought they would fare better as they traveled to Paris. She knew the danger they faced. Even though she would be devastated if they were harmed, she knew what she must do. Their loss was insignificant, when she considered the mayhem such men would let loose. The Abbess possessed tremendous courage!"

"What did the Reverend Mother do?" Eui sook

asked. She pictured the young novices of the Abbey, and was fascinated with the idea that only girls would save the Abbey.

Master Kija looked almost fondly at Eui sook. He understood her interest in the young women. "The only way to save the Service was to break it up. A unified Chataigne Service contained a force that defies the laws of nature and the understanding of men."

"Just like the *Taegeuk!*" Hee yung Kim waved his hand, excitedly.

"Yes," continued Master Kija. "Each of the eight women took one of the ornate pieces and traveled far away from each other. The Abbess instructed each of them. If any of the nuns were threatened, they were to take their pieces to Paris. Cecile and Genevieve would stay in Paris, where they would be sheltered by a friend of the Abbess, Cardinal Thoreaux. They would secret the pieces, safely.

"Why did they have to stay in Paris?" Eui sook persisted. "Wasn't it dangerous to be in Paris during the French Revolution?"

"The Abbess realized Cecile and Genevieve were young and physically able. They had not toiled for years in the Abbey gardens: had not spent years on their knees, scrubbing stone floors. Though young, the girls possessed wisdom. The most evil of the Freemasons suspected the Service was secretly buried within the walls of the Chataigne Abby. The Service and her novices would be safer right in the heart of the revolution, Paris. The Abbess believed the power of the Chataigne Service would protect the girls. Alas, the Abbess' hope did not fully materialize."

Eui Sook slapped her hands over her mouth. "Ooh, what happened?"

Master Kija did not want to explain the fate of the novices to the naïve, excitable Eui sook. He paused. He looked at Eui sook, and said quietly. "Amidst the tumult of the Revolution, rioting mobs were everywhere. Any beautiful, well-presented person was suspect. The ruffians grabbed Genevieve, and thrust her on the guillotine. Cecile threw herself atop Genevieve, trying to save her sister. The mob dragged Cecile away, and the guillotine released. Genevieve was beheaded!"

MYSTERIOUS EIGHT THROUGH THE AGES

The children were silent for a long moment. Master Kija watched them closely. He knew he jolted them with the story of the Chataigne Service. He hoped it would help each student understand the severity of each assigned mission. The seven young warriors, shocked into silence, sat still. Seven pairs of wide eyes fixed upon Master Kija. They stared at their old Master as if looking at a mysterious stranger. Greatly conflicted, Master Kija acknowledged their expressions.

"Good." He thought. "Each will stand a better chance of success and survival." Sadly, he also recognized, again, the end of innocence as each young face reflected a dawning of a harsh reality. "It is necessary!" he told himself. "Necessary!"

Chang nom Kim rallied first. Not knowing really what to say, he asked, "Are there more sacred eight stories?"

"These are not stories!" Master Kija quickly rose to his feet, and actually stamped a foot. "Ancient legends, based on the deeds and recitals of wise men are not stories! Historical yore is our real past, and in many cases, the birth of culture. The number eight is intrinsically wound through all of times past."

Master Kija sat back down and calmed himself. Perhaps more historical material would help the students gain a broader perspective. He again considered the history he knew. He talked of the ancient, immutable *I Ching*, or *Book of Changes*. The origins of the *I Ching* are lost in the mist of antiquity. Ancient historians accepted it as a Confucian text. The *I Ching* is comprised of eight divinations, called trigrams. The trigrams evolved, according to ancient lore, when illiterate peasants used yarrow stalks to determine the vigor of the year's harvest. The peasants forecast the future harvests by the arrangement of short and long stalks. Through time, this practice became part of the *I Ching*. The stalks became symbolized as trigrams; straight or broken lines, arranged in groups of three. Eight trigrams emerged, representing universal sentiments. Many years later, around the tenth century, the eight trigrams transformed into a circle, and laid the groundwork for the martial art, pa-kua.

An air of stillness caused Master Kija to pause. He had been speaking with his eyes closed. He shook his head and looked at his students. Eui sook had curled on her side and seemed to the asleep! She was probably dreaming of the French Abbess. Hee yung Kim was fiddling with the buttons on his vest. The other boys were sitting upright, but he could tell they were lost in some other sphere and were not thinking about the *I Ching*. Only Jung sup Kim seemed fully alert and engaged in the Master's dissertation of history.

"*Chariet!*" He commanded in a stern voice. The startled students sprang to alertness. Eui sook sat up quickly and rubbed her eyes.

"It is important," Master Kija began, as he straightened himself and eyed each child, "to talk about the 'Eightfold Path of the Buddha,' as it so closely parallels the *Taekeon* philosophy."

He spoke of Patanjali, author and recorder of the *Yoga Sutra*, which outlines the eight fundamental tenets of Yoga. Each of the eight limbs, or steps, represents a sequential stage in one's life journey. Students of Yoga, or Buddhism, would learn the tenets of the eight steps in precise order. In this way, the students reach full realization of the mental and spiritual aspects of each of the eight steps, or limbs. Only then, can the practitioner attain the ultimate goal of each discipline.

"Master Kija." Eui sook jumped to her feet. "What happened to the Abbess? What happened to the Abbess, Alouette Descoteaux? Did she return to the Abbey? Was the Chataigne Service actually saved?" Master Kija turned and looked at his smallest student with some sadness. He could not bring himself to answer her.

"No." The old master seemed to shrink into his garment. "I have talked for hours. I am weary. We have so much to do, and we cannot talk more. You understand," he looked at each of them, "what needs to be done. I am proud of your attentiveness, for I believe you now appreciate the urgency at hand."

THE SEARCH
OF THE CAVE

He rose to his feet on creaking knees. "I will rest a little while." He pointed at Jung sup Kim. "You will organize how we will conduct the search. Also, some of you stir the coals for we will need to eat." He slowly turned his back and headed for a pallet against a far wall.

"But, I thought you… " Hee yung Kim stuttered to his back.

"Tut!" Master Kija reached the pallet and melted into it. The students gathered to the opposite side, sank to the floor in an uneven circle and stared at each other.

It took many days to locate and recover the statuary, as the large cave opened into a myriad of further, smaller caves. Hee yung Kim wandered deeply into the caverns and became lost. His furious yells bounced back and forth around the caverns, further disorienting him, making it impossible for the others to find him. Some time was lost before answering echoes led him to safety. During these anxious days, it was necessary for one of the students to stand guard just beyond the entrance. Jung sup Kim worked this important and hazardous duty. On the second day Jung sup Kim descended the perilous trail and foraged food and tea from Sinuju and surrounding fields.

A full week passed for the children to recover seven statutes, containing the *kwaes*. They did not recover the statue containing *Pol jang Taegeuk* and its *kwae*. Master Kija decided one *kwae* could remain safely hidden in the Cave. The exhaustive search left each of them with blackened nails and hands covered in gray soil. Master Kija wasted no time, but immediately doled out brushes and cloths to clean the statutes.

"May we rest?" whined Eui sook. "I'm tired and hungry."

"We will eat some more of the kimchi and rice that Jung sup Kim gathered. We cannot tarry! Every day we take puts us in more danger." Master Kija's anxiety overrode hid his own weariness and hunger pains.

Their small stomachs replenished to some degree, the children attacked the tedious job of cleaning the statues. Gold and silver patinas emerged; precious jewels sparkled, as centuries old soot was scrubbed from the statues. "Oh, look how pretty!" Eui sook cried excitedly. Even the boys worked a little more eagerly as the beauty of each statue revealed itself.

Finally, the statues were ready. Master Kija arranged each according to the secret code in jewels on the statues. He placed the statues containing the *kwaes* in order of *the taegeuk, Il jang, Yi jang, Sam jang, Sa jang, O jang, Yuk jang, Chil jang*. The *Pol jang kwae* remained in a hidden location that he would later reveal to one of the children.

Pol-JANG
GAN
EARTH

Pol Jang represents Gan, or earth. Its kwae is three broken lines reflecting um, or negative energy, and lies directly below the kwae for heaven, which reflects yang, or positive energy. In the mortal cycle of life, Gan is both the ending of everything and the beginning of everything. This Taeguek is the highest poomse and transmits accuracy, power, and perseverance.

THE DISPERSION BEGINS

His gaze traveled over their heads, contemplating a sad realization. "I am devastated to put my students in such mortal danger. You are so young! Your training is incomplete. You are not the *Hwarang*. You must become a warrior like these ancient Silla warriors. You must breathe in their mystical spirit, their struggle against great odds. Like the *Hwarang*, you must endure!"

"I can be like the *Hwarang*," Hyun Cho responded, "I can run farther than any old soldier out there!" The other children sprawled tiredly on the dirt floor. Chin Ho, not to be outdone, shouted, "I can be like the *Hwarang*, too, but in this century!"

Master Kija managed a smile. "Yes, I feel sure you can outrun a mere soldier; even outfight a soldier with your martial arts skills. "That is not enough!" he exclaimed loudly. "You cannot outrun a their lorries. You cannot win a fight against a bullet!"

They each straightened their tired backs and looked at each other. Eui sook's eyes watered, again. Chang nom Kim's eyes widened even further. Jun sup Kim seemed to be searching inward, as if pondering a mystery. Chin Ho and Hyun Cho looked at each other with some mixture of trepidation and excitement.

Master Kija looked at Chul Moo, the only student whose eyes were fixed on him. He explained in a softer voice. "You will need the shield contained within the contents of the treasure you are saving."

Jung sup Kim questioned. "I thought the great power lie in the whole of the *Taegeuk* circle. Did you not say that?"

"Each *kwae* has its own force of nature," responded Master Kija. "To prevail in your mission, you must fully understand the meaning and breadth of the particular *kwae* you are saving." Again, he looked at each child, closely, appraising the unique qualities of each.

"There are two aspects to the *kwaes* that you must learn and understand. First, each *kwae* consists of three parallel lines. The top line represents the actuality of the *Taegeuk* form called a *poomse*. The *Taegeuk* is a pattern, a series of movements expressing many functions. Memory and application of the skill lead to an applicable defense. Each pattern of moves provides a counter attack. This is the stage each of you is at now."

They all nodded. Of course, they knew their *poomses* well.

"The middle line signifies the functional aspect of the substance, or object. What is Heaven? What is Joy? What is fire? What is the purpose of thunder? How does *Chil jang* relate to our mountain?" He paused and watched their faces. "You will need to comprehend these things."

"The bottom line is the most important to your success. This line represents the spiritual aspect. A solid line denotes perfection. A broken line reveals imperfections in that aspect. This line contains the mystical essence of the kwae. You must drink in, become the spirit!"

The Master had decided months ago that *Il Jang* must be the first *kwae* to be hidden far away. In many ways, the essence of perfection, represented by *Il Jang*, made it the most desirable of the *kwaes*. The Imperial leader of Japan might be mollified to gain only this, at least temporarily. The other Masters had agreed with Master Kija on this. They had also discussed Jung sup Kim, and agreed that he was the most likely child to start the diaspora of the *kwaes*. He was the oldest of the students, and, thankfully, the gravest. "Jung sup Kim possesses a trustworthy nature. He also must be the one to know where each idol is placed," Master Kija thought to himself.

IL-JANG
KEON
HEAVEN

This Taegeuk (poomse) is in the top position (12:00 o'clock) on the yin/yang circle. Il Jang represents Keon, the creation, the achievement of heaven. The three unbroken lines of its kwae impart perfection. The poomse is performed with simple, strong, and powerful movements.

Jung sup Kim
and *Il Jang Taegeuk*

"Jung sup Kim, please pack your knapsack and come before me." Master Kija carefully placed the statute containing the *Il jang kwae* into a leather pouch and pulled the leather straps tightly. Jung-sup Kim stood in front of him with his knapsack.

"I put a little of the rice and kimchi in my knapsack," he said.

"Good, good," Master Kija replied. "Now, tie this leather pouch to your belt. Your wide trousers will conceal it. You have in this pouch the idol containing the *kwae* for *Taegeuk Ill jang*. This kwae consists of three unbroken lines, and represents the *keon*, the *yang*: positive energy and the beginning of Creation. This *kwae* is the keystone to the *Taegeuk*. Remember, three unbroken lines represent perfection. The movements are simple, strong and powerful."

"First, you must go around Sinuju, to avoid the soldiers of Major Yamagata. You must circle west, through the forests, and then swing east toward the coast. You have many miles to travel through Korea to the south, and the large city of Daegu."

Jun sup Kim stared wordlessly at Master Kija, who continued. "A famous Buddhist Monk, Woncheuk, lives and writes in the Taigu Temple. Many students secretly practice their martial arts skills under Woncheuk, who is also a Master of *Tae Keon*. Master Woncheuk and I have corresponded. He will know how to take care of you and your statue."

"Master, aren't most of the Japanese based in the South, making it a more dangerous route?"

"There is a measure of safety in that fact. You must travel along the coast, on fishing vessels and ships that need laborers. When you reach the port of Pohang, a Taigu monk will meet you and transport you to the temple in a cart. He will recognize you. He will be carrying a large sack with yellow characters on it."

Master Kija placed his hand on Jun sup Kim's shoulder and drew him closer. "Now listen carefully and I will tell you how to use the power of *Il jang*." He explained, in quiet detail, the advantageous moves intrinsic in *Il Jang*. "Jung sup Kim," he whispered urgently. "You must allow yourself to have complete faith in the movements and the spirit of *Il jang*. When you find yourself in mortal danger, remember my words!" Jung sup Kim nodded, to frightened to speak. He picked up his knapsack.

Jung sup Kim went to each of his fellow students and said goodbye. Eui sook's tears ran down her cheeks and Chul Moo trembled as he shook his friend's hand. Master Kija watched the children with sad eyes. He saluted Jung sup Kim in the fashion of *Tae Keon*, and turned away.

Master Kija backed into the shadowy passage as the children were watching Jun sup Kim disappear into the darkness. Once again, he grabbed a small parchment square and penned his urgent message. Quickly, he affixed the parchment to a second pigeon. The bird hovered over Master Kija's palm for a second, and then spun up through the sunlit cleft.

Jung sup Kim slipped from the cave and began the treacherous climb down the mountain. He began his descent in the morning and by evening he reached a small plateau that marked the beginning of the trail. He slumped against a small boulder and his head fell to his knees. Too weary to lift his head, he fumbled blindly into his knapsack for food. As the pounding of his heart ebbed, the sound of footfalls pierced his consciousness. The footsteps tramped, with little attempt to move stealthily. Jung sup Kim whirled around and scrunched behind the boulder, which barely concealed him. Just as he gathered the folds of his trousers, he heard a voice.

"Hai, there is one of those wretched rapscallions! I've got him". The soldier lunged forward and dragged Jung sup Kim out from the boulder by his collar. A second soldier grabbed his right arm and twisted it behind his back. He could not move without extreme pain from his twisted arm. Jung sup Kim was terrified, frozen in the soldier's grip. Two more soldiers rushed forward to join their comrades and the captive. Jung sup Kim squirmed, ineffectively. The soldiers sneered.

Suddenly, Master Kija's words trickled through his panic. "When you lose the opportunity for pre-emptive strike, you must avoid an attack with a push, grab or strike." Just as Jung sup Kim thought, "How do I do that?" He turned into the soldier holding his arm. He blocked the offending arm and thrust his left hand around the soldier's neck and forced his head down. Jung sup Kim grabbed the soldier's left hand with his right. He turned sharply counterclockwise, forcing the soldier's head deeper and struck a hard blow to the base of the skull. The soldier collapsed. The surrounding men jumped back, startled by the young boy's swift reaction. Jung sup Kim whipped around to face the first soldier. This time, he rushed into the soldier with a forearm slap to his chest, and repeated the violent moves.

Gunshots rang out! A small cadre of soldiers rushed up, firing haphazardly. Bullets slammed into the boulders, showering Jung sup Kim with granite shards. Blood streamed down his face, and he could not see. "I cannot outrun a bullet," he thought desperately. He sank into a low stance and powered a blow into what he thought would be the midsection of the oncoming soldier. He still could not see. He hefted the soldier up, using his body as a shield, and backed into a thicket. With all his strength, he threw the soldier into the midst of his fellow warriors, squirming over each other to get at the boy. Jung sup Kim wriggled, backward, as far into the brush as he could. Shots pattered around him. He started to slide straight down.

"No," he said aloud. "I'll move sideways, toward the direction of the trail. They won't expect that." He slithered through the bush, reached the trail, rose up to cross it. Suddenly, rough hands grabbed his neck. A tardy soldier coming up the path quickly assessed the situation and cannoned into Jung sup Kim. Jung sup Kim threw up a left block to avoid a right punch. He grabbed the top of the soldier's head, forced it down, and delivered a strong kick to the face. The soldier fell to the ground, and Jun-sup Kim literally rolled him down the path. He crashed through the brush and stumbled as far as he could. The commotion of the searching solders hid his movements.

It was hours later when he finally slumped to his knees. He was utterly exhausted, but felt he had eluded the soldiers. Jung sup Kim's panic had driven him back up the mountain and he realized he was only a couple hundred yards from the entrance to his cave. He longed, desperately, to be back in the warmth and sanctity of the *dojang*.   His heart was willing, but his legs remained folded and his arms lay, helplessly, upon his knees.

"Now, what can I do?" he whispered to himself as he bowed his head. He felt the bulge of the leather pouch under his thigh. "What do I do now?" In his hard, young life he had never felt so desolate.

Faraway sounds penetrated his despair. He raised his head, and then quickly jumped to his feet.

"Oh no!"

Intermittent sparks of lamplight penetrated the darkness below him. The flashes of light seemed to be snaking upward, toward, not him, but easterly, in the direction of the *dojang*. It immediately struck him. The soldiers had discovered the trail!

Now he had no choice. He had to return to the cave and warn the others. Even though the soldiers could miss the boulder strewn hidden entrance, he could not chance it. Jun sum Kim summoned every fiber of strength into his young exhausted body and scampered up sheer rock faces.

Master Kija and Students Leave Their Cave

Bloody faced, in shredded mud stained clothes, Jung sup Kim flung himself through the cave entrance and collapsed on the hard ground. The other students screamed and grabbed each other. Jun sup Kim rolled deep into the cave and slowly rose to his hands and fee. With a great effort, he raised his head and sought out Master Kija. He did not see him. A deep sense of forsakenness pressed upon him. Jung sup Kim fought for his breath. The students stood around him in stunned silence.

Agonizing seconds later, he heard muffled footsteps as Master Kija rushed from the stone corridor and pushed through his students. Master Kija kneeled down and helped the distressed boy to his feet. "Tell us what happened. How did you manage to return here after all this time? You must have been to the bottom of the trail! What brought you back to the *dojang*?" His voice rang with distress, bordering on terror.

"The soldiers were amassed at the base of the mountain path. They grabbed me and I had to fight my way clear. They shot at me!"

Eui sook screamed again. "They shot bullets at you?" The other boys just stared at Jun sup Kim, with their mouths open.

Jung sup Kim fought to hold back his tears. "I only managed to escape because of the darkness and the confusion of the soldiers. But now they have found the trail! I could see the lanterns below me."

"You fought against soldiers and guns and survived. I am proud of you! You could have escaped back down the mountain, but you came to warn us instead. I am proud of you, Jung sup Kim," Master Kija repeated quietly. "You are right. We cannot allow the soldiers to discover our cave. Now, our plans have changed only slightly. We must move immediately. "

"Eui sook and Chang nom Kim dampen the fire, quickly, before any light somehow escape. Chin Ho, put lids on the kimchi and rice and carry them into the corridor. Hyun Cho, help Chin Ho shove the stones in front of the opening to the corridor."

Jung sup Kim, still collapsed on the ground, gasped as Master Kija dropped to his knees and began tearing at the mats. The tranquil Master had transformed into a powerful general, issuing decisive orders. Could he have been preparing for such a moment?

"Chul Moo, help me roll up the matting. Wait, Hyun Cho! We need to store the mats in first."

Hee yung Kim was already using a twig broom to sweep away evidence of footprints. "Hee yung Kim, throw rocks and dirt into the fire pit."

Master Kiji began feeling his way along the rock walls, gathering any evidence of *Tae Keon* activities, and rolling the papers tightly. "Chul Moo, help me reach the flag!"

"Now children," he said in the darkening cave, "quickly gather your knapsacks and leather pouches containing the statues." He stood near the entrance, where the lighter outside night shadowed him. The children scampered around the dark cave and retrieved their belongings. In one voice they finally said, "We are ready."

"Follow me." The old man, moved like a preying tiger. Swiftly, unwaveringly, he slid through the cave entrance. The children flew through the opening. They barely saw Master Kija's ghostly figure fleeing up an unknown route. Jung sup Kim trailed last. He hunched his shoulders and darted uneasy looks behind him. Sounds of gunshots still echoed through his head. After a while, he realized that he and his fellow escapees were wrapping back toward the trail, and going downhill.

Master Kija disappeared under a low ledge so quickly and silently that only Hyun Cho, first in line, saw him. One by one, each followed the disappearing child in front, until they found themselves in a round cave like space, but with no ceiling. Stars twinkled merrily above them, belying the terrifying tableau on the mountain below them.

Hyun Cho and *Yi Jang*

The children looked up to the sky and then around the open cave. They gathered in a tight knot, each holding on to their knapsacks. Each of them had tied the leather pouches to their belts as they had seen Jung sup Kim do. Not one of them spoke or moved.

"Here is our plan," Master Kija began without preamble. "Hyun Cho, listen carefully. You are to take the pouch containing the *Yi jang*." At these words, each child reached into trousers to identify the *Yi jang* pouch. It so happened that Hyun Cho already had it tied to his belt.

"I am sure that you know of the old trader in Sinuju called Dae Ho." They all nodded.

"The Japanese allow Dae Ho to keep his mule and cart so he can carry provisions to their bases. They do not know of his real expertise. Old Dae Ho knows every trail and footpath in the rugged mountains of the Changbai Range. He will guide you east, across the mountains, to Port Songjin, on the Sea of Japan. Port Songjin is his family home, so he will leave you there. At the port, you will have to steal a boat. It must be a decrepit boat, but a strong boat. It must be strong enough to carry you south, to the city of Hungnam."

They looked bewilderingly at each other. Not even the inquisitive Hee yung Kim could summon the strength to question their Master. How did the Master know all these details? How long had he been making these plans?

"The *Taegeuk*, *Yi Jang*, represents *tae*," the Master continued. "*Tae* signifies internal firmness and external softness. Like your boat, you will not appear to be a threat to anyone. You will look like a poor, disreputable, fisher, living a sad existence on the seacoast. Your strength and courage, necessary to this mission, will go unnoticed. About one hundred miles down the coast you will see the city, Hungnam. Tie your boat at the pier, and immediately lose yourself in the city. This is important. You must seek the sanctuary, Jinheung, immediately."

"How do I find the sanctuary?" asked Hyun Cho, struggling to hide his fear.

Master replied, patiently. "You will appear to be a poor waif, or orphan, not unlike many Korean children." He suddenly straightened and pointed his finger a Hyun Cho. "Do not approach the Japanese! Look for a sensible looking Korean. I believe that any Korean adult could not but help a poor child. Also, I am sure that most Koreans know of the Jinheung sanctuary."

Master Kija lowered his hand and tried to smile at Hyun Cho. "At the sanctuary, you will meet Dong sun Lee. He is a Confucianist, and a brave Korean, and he will know what to do. Dong sun Lee will see that the statue containing *Yi jang* is safely hidden. You must remain in the sanctuary until it is safe to return home.

We have made extensive plans for your return to Sinuju once it is safe.

They all spoke at once. "Do you know the sanctuary person?" and "All those miles by oneself?" Hyun Cho's voice rose over the others. "I am to come home, then? What plans, and with whom?"

"Tut," admonished Master Kija. "Did I not tell you of many years of planning?"

Then Hyun Cho stepped close to Master Kija, and spoke in a wavering voice. "My family, what about my family? The Japanese might notice I have gone and think I have joined the rebels. They might be punished."

"You have joined the rebels, " Master Kija replied softly. "We all have. We are a different kind of rebel, entrusted with a vitally important mission. I cannot tell you that the Japanese will not notice that several children in Sinuju have suddenly disappeared. They know of only one rebel, so far, and that is Jung sup Kim. I simply do not know what Major Yamagata and his soldiers will do. I only know what we must do."

"It is astonishing," thought Jung sup Kim. "Master Kija has shed his years and become a Warrior Chief. His face and voice are calm, yet strong. One would think he is teaching a *poomse* move, rather than leading us through danger."

"Hyun Cho." Master Kija spoke as if he heard no outburst. "You are a strong, well trained boy. We must believe that you will reach the sanctuary and complete the mission of saving *Yi jang*. We must believe that your family is strong and will endure whatever Major Yamagata may do. To believe otherwise is simply nonproductive."

Hyun Cho tied his pouch tightly to his belt and saluted the other children. "I will slip down the mountain on a goat path to avoid the soldiers. I know where Dae Ho's hut is. We use to tease him and his mule."

"There is more I must say before you go," Master Kija replied. "Children, we must be quiet!"

Master Kija and Hyun Cho sat in lotus position facing each other and apart from the others. The Master spoke in whispered tones for some minutes. Master Kija rose again on stiff legs, and the children heard him say. "When faced with danger, remember my words! Use the strength and joy inherent in your *Taegeuk*."

Hyun Cho saluted again and slipped through the cave opening.

SAM-JANG

RA

FIRE

The Taeguek Sam Jang represents Ra, or fire. Its kwae consists of a broken line encased with two solid lines. Intensity, heat and brilliance are unconstrained when passion, accompanied by training, is set ablaze.

Hee Yung Kim leaves with *Sam Jang*

"Hee Yung Kim," he continued, "You will take the statue containing *Sam jang* to a safe refuge. I feel you personally possess passion and intensity, the essences inborn in this *Taegeuk*. *Sam jang* is *Ra*, or fire. It possesses heat and brilliance. This is the first *poomse* to emphasize counterattacks."

"You will proceed southwest, following the Yalu River to the flood plains along the west coast. Once you reach the rice paddies, you must turn south. There are many roads going into Seoul, so you may be able to hitch a ride."

Again, a chorus of anxious questions echoed around the small cave. "He's going into Seoul?" "That is the headquarters for the soldiers!" "He will be caught!" Eui sook wailed.

"Tut!" Master Kija. "We are trapped, here, in this cave if this persists," he whispered harshly. He rose, tall and stern. "Did you forget the enormous risk we are undertaking? Did you forget?" They bunched together, chastened, mute.

"Hee yung Kim is quick. He will easily learn to use

the offensive moves introduced in *Sam Jang*. We will wrap a bloodied rag around Hee yung Kim's head, and devise a sling for his arm. He will keep his eyes blank, as if senseless, and appear unfit for subscription into Japanese camps. Farmers' may take pity on him, and give him a ride." He looked sharply at the bunched group. No one made a sound.

"In the *Sam Jang* kwae a broken line is encased with two solid lines. Hee yung Kim's passion, like *Ra*, will lie suppressed until it is called for. *Ra* is fire. He must heed the divine guidance of *Sam Jang*. For when the fire blazes, it produces a tremendous power."

"You understand the restraint and caution you must use?" Master Kija looked at Hee yung Kim. It was more a command than a question. Hee yung Kim nodded.

"Now, you will go to the Doseonsa Temple at the foot of Mount Samgaksan. It will be easy to find. It is the largest Buddhist center in Korea, and takes up many acres. The code word at the interior gate is Jinul, the name of an ancient Buddhist leader. The monk at the gate will take you to the Buddhist Acharya. Acharya will relieve you of the statue, keep you safe thereafter, and become your mentor. You must stay in the Temple, as a novice, until it is safe to roam the streets as a Korean."

Master Kija beckoned Hee yung Kim to his side. They sat down, facing each other with their knees touching. For several minutes, the youngster listened to the soft instructions. Then, in a voice they all heard, "When you think there is no way to avoid danger, remember my words!"

Master Kija and Hee yung Kim ducked out of the cave, and the children listened to night sounds in the faint glow of the stars.

They did not hear him return, and jumped up at his sudden reappearance. "How will you know that he arrived at the temple safely?" asked Chin Ho. "How can he go all that way, alone?" Eui sook sobbed.

"Hee yung Kim carries with him the strength of *Sam Jang*. He will listen to it with his heart and carry out the divinations with great force. Acharya will be expecting him."

"Now, gather close." Master Kija sat down, facing the small entrance, and the remaining children clustered around him.

"I heard distant sounds of troops. We must whisper and make no noise and ask no more questions. These arrangements have been years in the making. You must trust them."

He continued. "Chin Ho and Eui sook will travel together. Chin Ho will carry the vessel containing *O Jang*. Eui sook will carry *Sa jang*. Eui sook is younger and slighter than the rest of you, and will need a strong spiritual force to accompany her. *Sa jang* represents *Jin*, which is thunder and signifies power and courage."

They could barely see his tender smile in the soft light. "Eui sook, do not sob and weep when you encounter danger. Conjure the force of *Sa jang*. You will loosen a thunderous din and roil the earth beneath your assailants."

"Chin Ho, a great force will accompany you in the *kwae of O Jang*. *O Jang* represents *Seon*, the paradox of air. *Seon* embodies the might of a powerful gale, as well as the stillness of no wind. This paradox reflects the strength and weakness inherent in all things. When you exercise the capacity of a strong wind, you exercise a great power. When you understand the breadth of that power, you acquire calmness. "

"The two of you are embarking on the longest journey. You will need the force of *Jin* and the enigma of *Seon*. Chin Ho, I have special papers for you. Because you are tall, the Japanese will notice you and try to conscript you. These papers confirm that as a citizen of Kangyung, you have leave to deliver your orphaned sister to a convent near Makpo. Then you are to return to Kangyung and report to the Japanese army post."

Master Kija sighed and looked down at Eui sook, who, amazingly, had dry eyes.

Chin Ho gasped as he glanced at the papers. "Jeju! Why that is all the way through Korea. It will take us months! We have no money for food. Where will we stay?"

"Tut!" Master Kija raised his palm impatiently. "Details are handled! You, also, will travel to Seoul. The Japanese built a railway that begins in Seoul, and is now finished all the way to Kwangju. You will need your papers to board the railway. The train is slow and tedious, but is the only practical way to the Southern part of Korea. In Kwangju, you should be able to catch a ride on a farmer's bullock's cart to the coastal town of Mokpo.

There is a large pier in Mokpo. You will need to use your papers again to board the ferry that moors there. This ferry trolls around the islands off the coast and will deliver you to the island of Jeju. The ferry lands at the port of Seogwipo. As of yet, the Japanese have little presence on the island. It is sixty miles from the mainland. Jeju Island's economy centers around fishing, and women fishers and divers. As soon as you depart the ferry, Chin Ho, you must find a strand of kelp and drape it around your neck. A Haenyeo, a female diver, will be watching for you."

Master Kija reached under his vest and drew out a small leather pouch tied to his trouser belt. He shook several gold coins out of the pouch, and handed them to Chin Ho, without speaking. Chin Ho, too, was speechless, and he took the coins.

Suddenly, a loud clatter sounded outside their cave. They all crouched defensively, their eyes darting to the small entrance of their shelter. Master Kija reacted instantly. "We cannot be trapped here!" He whisked through the opening and fled down a path, only he could see. Quick as a mouse, Eui sook whirled through the opening after him. The four boys followed, barely in time to see Eui sook's pale vest disappearing around a string of boulders.

They stumbled over roots and stones, desperate to follow Master Kija, who seemed to glide above the path. Eui sook, swifter than the boys, floated in his wake. They wound around the dark, rough mountainside for miles, until Master Kija stopped, suddenly, by a blackened tree stump. The children plunked down on their backsides to keep from slithering over the stones past the Master.

"Chin Ho, Eui sook," Master Kija panted. "You must

take the path that diverges from ours." He pointed to a small opening of boulders in the blackness. He realized they had not been fully prepared, as has Hyun Cho and Hee yung Kim. He only had time for a final admonition. "Hear my voice. When you are in harm's way, let my voice recall the forces of the *kwaes* you carry. You must trust, and mindlessly follow these forces, and you will prevail. Go now."

Again, Eui sook took off in a flash down the offshoot path. Chin Ho hesitated a second, then ran after her.

Chil-JANG
KAN

MOUNTAIN

The kwae for Chil Jang consists of two broken lines topped by an unbroken line and is placed on the yin/yang circle opposite the Yi Jang kwae. Chil Jang means mountain, Kan, which reflects majesty, and stability. Above all, contained within its ponderous firmness is wisdom.

Chang nom Kim and *Chil Jang*

Master Kija wheeled around and sped down the path. Chang nom Kim and Chul Moo followed closely. Jung sup Kim, sore and weakened, limped after them. A while later, Jung sup Kim realized that the path had merged into the familiar trail they used to ascend to their cave. He was too weary to question Master Kija, and grateful to be on familiar footing.

"Hai!" Jung sup Kim jolted to a stop and opened his eyes. He had been walking blindly. Now he could see Master Kija and Chang nom Kim, standing with their arms raised, surrounded by Japanese soldiers. Prodded in the back by rifle, he limped to Chang nom Kim's side and raised his hands.

The soldiers poked their captives with fixed bayonets. Chang nom-Kim edged close to Master Kija and spoke quietly. "Please tell me about *Chil jang*, Master."

"You know," started Master Kija, looking straight ahead. "Oh, you just started learning *Chil jang*."

"I know the movements," Chang nom Kim whispered. "I need to know the meaning, as you told Jung sup Kim about *Il jang*" and Hyun Cho about *Ye Jang*."

Master Kija, walking stiffly in front of the prodding bayonet, looked down at his frail student close beside him. Neither could stop on the narrow path and Chang nom Kim moved to the front of Master Kija. His large eyes looked back at the Master with a fixed determination. "Please tell me!" Chang nom Kim pleaded.

Before Master Kija could reply Chang nom Kim acted. He realized the prodding soldiers were behind the Master, and that he was behind the forward marching soldier. He rushed forward in a spurt of dust. Alerted, the soldier spun around and attempted to raise his fixed bayonet. Chang nom Kim slapped the rifle aside with his right hand and grabbed the soldier's right arm with his left. He twisted the soldier's arm around and pressed his head down with his right elbow. Then, pinned down with the arm bar, the soldier shielded Chang nom Kim from his comrades, who brushed Master Kija aside, and rushed forward. Chang nom Kim backed slowly down the trail, kicking the pinned soldier in the face, left foot, right foot.

"No!" Master Kija wailed, and attempted to push through the surging soldiers and reach Chang nom Kim. He managed to squeeze through the soldiers and grab Chang nom Kim's arm. The skinny arm slipped Master Kija's grasp. "Hai!" the beaten guard choked and fell flat, leaving both the Master and his student exposed to the angered guard. A second guard rushed forward, his rifle and fixed bayonet raised.

"No, " Master Kija shouted again. "Stop"

"Shut up!" The guard shoved Master Kija aside. Chang nom Kim quickly drew back his left leg, while simultaneously sweeping across the soldiers body with a right hand palm strike. The rifle and bayonet swung out to the soldier's right side. Master Kija somehow managed to stagger forward, grabbed the rifle, and twisted it free. Chang nom Kim launched a vicious right front kick to the soldier's groin. He followed it up with a solid left hook to the temple. The soldier dropped low and swept his bayonet upward. A vivid red crescent started at Chang nom Kim's stomach and curved cruelly across his chest.

Two more soldiers moved in and slammed Master Kija to the ground. Chang nom Kim reacted violently, mindless of his ruptured body. He turned to the soldier on his right and threw his right palm into the upper arm. Chang nom Kim's palm continued up and around the soldiers arm. With his left hand, Chang nom Kim forced the soldier's arm up behind, and bent his body forward. Chang nom Kim twisted violently to the left and rammed the soldier's bent head into other soldier. But now, he was spent. His body gushed blood from the brutal wound.

"Tell me, Master," shouted the weakened, bloodied student. Two more soldiers grabbed his legs. "Tell me!"

"You are a mountain!" Master Kija, with a dreadful sense of doom. He was overcome with both, love and fear, for his young, valiant warrior. 'Your formidable strength equals that of an army.' He clumsily got to his feet. "You are resolute, loyal and brave!"

Jung sup Kim and Master Kija, both wounded, weakly pried at the arms and legs of Chang nom Kim's attackers. Chang nom Kim grabbed his attacker by the neck, drawing the head down. His blood splattered everywhere. He plowed his knee into the soldiers face. He released the soldier's neck, and punched his midsection with both fists. The soldier doubled over. Chang nom Kim crossed his forearms and brought an x strike down on the soldier's neck, breaking it. Chang nom Kim turned, found his Master's eyes and fearlessly smiled into them. "I am a mountain! I am earth and power!" The first bullet slammed into his chest.

Two soldiers dragged Chang nom Kim's bloodied body, by his feet, down the trail. Dust swirled behind them, enveloping the dazed, distraught Master Kija. His tears ran though the caked dust. The soldiers pushed him brutally forward. Jung sup Kim limped behind, prodded by bayonet. He was in shock. He couldn't believe what happened. How did the frail Chang nom Kim become a paragon of strength, a hero? Did he really breathe in the power of *Chil jang*? Jung sup Kim shivered as he remembered the crushing impact of the bullets on Chang nom Kim's small, battered body. Suddenly, he looked up, and around. He whispered to himself. "Where is Chul Moo?"

The soldiers marched Master Kija and the dispirited Jung sup Kim into Sinuju. Their fellow villagers watched quietly. The bloodied body, carelessly flung onto a wood shelf, rendered them mute. The soldiers threw the captured old man and boy into a small home they had commandeered just north of the village. They dragged Master Kija to his feet, slammed him against the hard earthen wall, and trussed his arms and feet. They did not bother to bind Jung sup Kim, who sprawled, unmoving, like a straw filled doll. The soldiers left the hut, slammed and barred the door. Jung sup Kim raised his head and looked at Master Kija. His arms were stretched painfully behind him and he raised his head slightly to see Jung sup Kim. "Where is ?" Jung sup Kim stopped because Master Kija, his eyes blazing, shook his head from side to side.

Yi-JANG
TAE
LAKE

The Yi Jang Taegeuk presents Tae, or lake. The kwae (in the 1:00 o'clock position on the yin/yang circle) is composed of a broken line atop two unbroken lines, which signifies outer softness and internal firmness. Inner strength and indomitable spirit lie beneath apparent weakness.

YADOOL

Hyun Cho and *Yi Jang*

When Hyun Cho and Dae Ho finally emerged from the foothills of the Changbai Range and trudged through the farmlands near the coast, they were almost unrecognizable. The man and boy were wretchedly thin. Hyun Cho's black hair was matted, greasy, and entangled with leaves and pieces of debris from sleeping on the ground. He plodded like an old man, his head down. The real old man walked erect. Dae Ho was no more than a skeleton, knotted with sinewy muscles. He strode firmly, and happily now, through his beloved home territory. Hyun Cho slumped behind him.

Hyun Cho squinted up at the wide bright sky, unbroken by the dark canopy of forest. Hyun Cho was grateful to be alive. He grew up in the shadow of Mt. Paektu and had never been afraid to play in the dark forests, which nestled at its base. Hyun Cho, and all the villagers, believed the sacred mountain protected them. He and his friends frolicked at will within the cold, dank forest throughout their childhood. The multitude of tigers, bears and other wild animals that also dwelled in those forests were respected, but not strongly feared.

This journey differed vastly from his childhood experience in the mountains. Fear haunted every stage of their flight across the mountain range. The almost barren mountaintops resembled alien planets and the forests were now dark and sinister to the young boy. The whole experience was foreign to him. He never before actually had to flee like a bandit through unfriendly, jungle like woods. The two escapees scaled hundreds of cliff faces, and stumbled along miles with scarce food and no rest. The mule died a day after their departure when he slid off a steep path and into a chasm, taking the cart with him. Hyun Cho was certain he would also be dead, if he were alone. Dae Ho unerringly followed nonexistent paths. He brought down small game with an old musket gun. He made fire with sticks, and managed to find shelter among rough stony ledges. Dae Ho climbed and descended with a steady gait, unhampered by Hyun Cho's weight as he clung to the back of the old man's jacket.

Finally, they reached the outskirts of the port town, Songjin. Dae Ho stopped abruptly near a rocky path that meandered northward, away from the port itself. He looked for long minutes at the sunken-cheeked boy, who now was gazing around the landscape with some apprehension. Hyun Cho became aware of Dae Ho's solemn contemplation. He straightened and took the hand offered by the old man. Dae Ho gravely clasped both hands around the boy's hand. He said Hyun Cho had been a brave and worthy traveling companion. Then he turned slowly, and started up the path. His head was facing the sky, as if beseeching some unknown deity to take over his job of protecting the boy.

Hyun Cho did not feel brave or worthy. He took a

painful breath and started to say just that, but Dae Ho was already a fast diminishing figure. He was on his own. Taking a deep, steadying breath, Hyun Cho continued the sloped road toward Songjin. "I can only go forward," he muttered to himself in a continuing mantra.

Hung Cho hiked slowly through the central market of the fishing village. Though not really a city or even a town, Songjin was much larger than Sinuju. The shops were too many, and too diverse, to count. They hugged tightly together with yawning open fronts. The throngs of people, pushing importantly to one place or another, fascinated Hung Cho. No one seemed to note his appearance as strange. He must, he thought, be just another dirty and unkempt boy.

He wandered through the market and up a small rise between the rustic buildings. He froze. He looked, shocked, at a world he had never imagined. The horizon stretched into infinity. As far as he could see, and he turned his head both ways, was grey upon grey. He could not tell the water from the sky. Everything moved. Grey rolled into light gray, which curled again into darker shade of gray. Some gray curls had extremely light gray tips, which sprayed and created lighter movements upon the large movements. It was a living, violent grey, which crashed, thundered, moaned and hissed. Hyun Cho was, simultaneously, terrified and hypnotized

"Master Kija wants me to steal a boat and go out into this nothingness," he thought in wonderment. "This sea does not reflect a soft exterior, and firm interior," as he recalled Master Kija's words. "I will be swallowed by the vastness, and become a minute piece of gray flotsam."

He turned and fled back to the relative safety of the crowded market. He spent the night curled behind a trash bin in the market place alley. He covered his ears, but the tumult of the water grew louder in the darkness. He spent two days and nights rummaging for food and sleeping in concealed corners. When he finally felt recovered from his trek, Hyun Cho considered his next move. He stole some clothes from drying lines and exchanged his ragged clothes. He carefully tied the leather pouch inside the unfamiliar trousers. He kept his back to the sea, ate and slept. "I must go forward," he kept repeating, but still could not face the unsettling sight that lie just over that small rise.

He awoke on the third day, sat up and cradled the leather pouch containing the *kwae* for *Yi jang*. "Maybe, if I rub the statue a genie will pop up, and tell me what to do." He recalled Master Kija's words. "The complete Taegeuk is spiritual, mythical and powerful. The Japanese must never gain that power, for they will use it in evil ways." My mission is to hide the *Yi jang kwae*, he thought to himself. "Within the *kwae* is the power to protect me. No! I must protect it." Hyun Cho shook his head side to side in mute anguish.

He gathered his courage and walked again between the buildings and out onto the beach. Once more, he faced an amazing vista. The sky was blue. The water was darker blue. Sunshine peeked in and out of fluffy white clouds. The giant waves rolled gently onto the sand. A mild salt-laden breeze wafted toward him. The seascape was not terrifying, but mesmerizing. To the south, a large pier jutted out into the sea. He had not seen it before in all the fog. Various boats were moored to the pier. He strolled onto the pier, munching the last of stolen rice cakes.

Several fishermen, and other boat people, he did not know what to call them, worked or sat on the pier. No one paid attention to him. Most of the people were facing the north. Hyun Cho walked up and down the South side of the pier. He tried to evaluate the five or six boats below him. He had never been in a boat. What was the difference between a good boat and a bad boat? Hyun Cho thought that a good boat would not sink, and dump him into the enormous water. One medium sized boat looked sturdy, with wide boards, and a small three-sided shelter at one end. It even had an engine, in addition to a sail. Hyun Cho knew a something about engines. In Sinuju, he watched the Japanese soldiers, as they continually had to tinker with their lorries. He examined the interior of the shelter closely and noted fuel cans lined up inside. He looked around and saw no one looking back.

Hyun Cho jumped into the sturdy boat. He opened a box tied in front of the steering bar and saw a wool blanket and some cans of food. Good. He stood on the prow and reached up to untie the mooring. A rough brown hand clamped down on his hand. .

"What are you doing?" A fat, brown man loomed large and angry above him.

"I, I," Hyun Cho stuttered. Before he could actually

say anything, the man picked Hyun Cho up by his arm, and threw him into the water. Hyun Cho swallowed a mouthful of water and bobbed toward the surface. Only, he could not surface. The man wedged a long pole against Hyun Cho's chest and held him underwater. He thrashed violently but the man merely pressed harder with the pole. His chest felt explosive. He panicked. He was drowning.

Mercifully, a vision of Master Kija's serene, seamed face arose before him. Hyun Cho stopped struggling and forced his body to relax. He heard the big man laugh as he floated, eyes closed, to the surface. The man dug his pole sharply into Hyun Cho's chest again. Hyun Cho exploded from the water, grabbed the pole with his right hand, forced the man down to his knees, and bent him over the pier. Hyun Cho tightened his right hand grip, and shot himself up, level with his attacker's head. As he rose, he swung his left arm out and delivered a powerful elbow strike to the man's head. He wrapped his left arm around the head and let go of the pole. His right hand freed, he dug his thumb into the crook of the man's right arm. Hyun Cho's right hand pushed the arm down. His left hand pulled on the man's neck. This push-pull force plunged the man into the water and Hyun Cho splashed down beside him.

Hyun Cho kicked free and dove to the other side of the boat. The man sputtered loudly, and emitted great squeals. A couple of men came over and looked down. At first, they laughed and pointed at the fat man, splashing helplessly. Belatedly, one of them threw a rope down to him. The fat man grabbed the rope but they could not pull him up. They dragged him toward the beach. While they were preoccupied, Hyun Cho, unnoticed, slithered over the boat edge and sat on the box of supplies. He pumped the engine furiously, grabbed the same pole, floating next to the boat, and braced it against one of the pier legs. The boat turned slowly, the engine sputtered, and he motored away from the pier. He could hear the struggling fat man and his laughing friends.

The 100 miles promised by Master Kija seemed to be 10,000 miles to the young sailor. Hyun Cho huddled, dreadfully seasick, on the bottom of his craft for three days. There was nothing else he could do but cling to the tiller, and hope he would not be flung into the sea. He realized right away that the small engine was no match for the immense strength of the waves. He was at the mercy of the wind and tides. The rough water tossed the little boat from crest to crest, dumped him, jarringly, into the bottom of each swell, but moved it inexorably south.

On the fourth morning, Hyun Cho awoke to the sight of a large city. Hungnam was much larger than the port of Songjin. He allowed the surf to push him to shore. He climbed from the boat and sank immediately to the sand. His legs could not stand. He sat and looked around. The multiple piers hummed with industrial sounds of fishing, hauling, and marketing. Flat bed trucks rambled on and off the piers. Two and three story buildings and giant markets made large city noises of their own. The noise of city life competed with the booming waves of the sea.

For many hours, Hyun Cho simply sat on the sand. How was one to lose oneself in this Hungnam metropolis? He wasn't sure how to get past the piers and into the city. After some time, he noticed an old woman sitting alone on the sand under the nearest pier. She sat still among an assortment of bags, boxes, and some kind of small cage. An odd sort of bicycle stood behind her.

She seemed to be looking at Hyun Cho. That was strange! He rose to his feet and retrieved his sandals and items he could carry from the boat. He carefully adjusted his clothes and secured the leather pouch tightly again to his belt. He plodded across the sand, entered the shade of the pier, and stopped a few feet from the woman.

"Is this the city of Hungnam?" he asked

"Of course," she replied. She looked at him steadily. "What a courageous young man. I am glad you made the trip successfully." The many wrinkles on her face shifted, and he thought she might be smiling.

"Are you expecting me?" he asked in an astonished whisper.

"Yes, Hyun Cho." The old woman rose, bowed over her left arm with right arm offered, in the way martial artists greet each other. "I am Chin Mae. I have been waiting many days on this beach for you to arrive. You used the might of *Yi jang* wisely, I see.

Hyun Cho rocked back, as though struck. "I am to meet some else," he blurted, "a person at the Jinheung sanctuary; a good person."

"Yes, he was a good man." Chin Mae began gathering her belongings. "The Japanese murdered Dong sun." She averted her face and began tying her things on the odd contraption. "The Japanese also set fire to the sanctuary, and, and." She whirled around, raised both hands in a helpless gesture. "They tried to kill all of his students and residents! Thankfully, many of them escaped through the back alley!"

Hyun Cho sank to his knees. "No, no," he cried. "Why?"

"Do those heathen need a reason?" she said bitterly. "The Japanese work hard to abolish our beliefs. They want to erase all signs Korean culture, and replace it with their own. They not only want to destroy our present, but erase our past. Dong sun refused to accept Shintoism, as the only religion. He also refused to turn away any needy person from the sanctuary."

"What will I do?" Hyun Cho cried, thinking only of himself. Chin Mae watched him thoughtfully. Distressed, he continued. "Master Kija said the *Taegeuk Yi jang* means inner strength and will. He also said that indomitable spirit, not forcefulness, is the gift of its *kwae*. What am I to do?" he said again. "I did not summon inner strength, because now I am lost."

Chin Mae talked faster, and a little impatiently. "How do you think you came all this way? What other young boy do you know could travel hundreds of miles alone? What other boy could jump into the sea, even though terrified by its strangeness?" She picked up his things and thrust them into his arms. "You had the strength and spirit to persevere. You embraced the life force of the *Yi jang.*"

Chin Mae turned to the present. "We must hurry.

You will stay with me, and together we will hide the *Yi jang kwae* in a safe place near the lake shore."

"I am to return to my village." Chin Mae grabbed his arm again. "No, this plan has changed. It is far too dangerous for you to be on the road without the guidance of Dong sun."

They spoke no more. Chin Mae supported Hyun Cho's tired young body as they walked and wheeled her strange bike along the beach. They skirted the city of Hungnam and began to climb the foothills of Mt. Samgakbong. Finally, they came to a small wooded glen, just before the ground rose sharply up the mountainside. The old woman and boy approached a tiny cabin sitting in a clearing. It was late and dark. As they climbed up the stoop, Hyun Cho could see the sparkled reflection of the full moon in a near lake. He dropped his exhausted body into a wooden rocking chair. His eyelids closed. He dreamt he saw Chin Mae step onto the porch and release a small bird from its cage, which hovered for a second, then shot high into the sky.

SAM-JANG
RA
FIRE

The Taeguek Sam Jang represents Ra, or fire. Its kwae consists of a broken line encased with two solid lines. Intensity, heat and brilliance are unconstrained when passion, accompanied by training, is set ablaze.

Hee yung Kim – *Sam Jang*

At the time Hyun Cho slept on Chin Mae's porch, his friend, Hee yung Kim, also slept. He was nestled deep in a prickly bed of fodder in a lumbering cart, pulled by two fat bullocks. A farmer of indeterminate age sat on the front bench with leather reins wrapped around his fists. He, too, was asleep. So far, Hee yung Kim's trek was uneventful. His disguise was effective. For the most part, Koreans had avoided him. Sadly, they turned away from the wounded boy, lest they be noticed, and singled out by the Japanese soldiers. The Japanese sentries dismissed him as injured, and therefore useless. He traveled many miles with this farmer, who happened to be traveling south, also. The farmer, luckily, took pity on the limping dull-eyed boy. The bullocks plodded along the worn, familiar road. The full moon created a brightness that competed with daylight.

A loud sputtering of engines split the quiet night. The farmer awoke instantly. "Quick," he said in a surprisingly commanding voice. "Burrow deeper into the vegetables, and do not make a sound!" Hee yung Kim wriggled down as far as he could, and hurriedly arranged the cart's contents on top of him. The clatter grew louder, and two soldiers, on small motorbikes, whizzed by, slowed, and then turned and blocked the road ahead.

"Old man, why are you traveling in the middle of the night?" They climbed off their bikes and stood aggressively in the path of the bullocks.

"Why, I am delivering vegetables to the city market." The farmer's voice returned to meekness. "Is it night? I confess I fell asleep, and did not notice the time passing."

"That sounds suspicious to me." The larger soldier fixed his bayonet on his rifle. "There is notice of a renegade crossing these fields. I am in charge of this section, and no guerilla will get by me."

"Why, you can see it is only I and my unworthy bullocks. They are slow and I have to make up the time." The farmer shrugged his shoulder.

"We will see!" The younger soldier jumped onto the cart. Hee yung Kim choked as the soldier's weight bore down on the cart's harvest. The soldier lifted his bayonet high and plunged it through the bags. The blade came just past the nose of Hee yung Kim, and he scrunched tighter and tried to work further into the cart. The farmer jerked sharply and looked back toward the cart. He struggled to erase the alarm from his face. Anything he did to help the boy now would only put both of them in deeper jeopardy.

The soldier was not satisfied with his test, and irritated with the apparent indifference of the old farmer. So, he tromped into the middle of the cart. With a sneering grunt, he raised his bayonet high, and plunged it into the cart again. The blade drove into the flesh of Hee yung Kim's right thigh. Pain ruptured through him. His body jerked and quenched uncontrollably. He smothered an agonized cry.

The farmer turned, his face impassive again, and watched the bayonet rip clear of the bags. He saw the stained blade, and stiffened. The soldier jumped from the cart, not yet inspecting the blade. The soldiers slapped their right hands together; laughing at the younger's audacity. So far the night's work of patrolling the dusty road had been boring. The diversion of this old farmer provided some amusement.

The farmer began to wave his arms. He wanted their attention on them, rather than the bloodied blade. "You have ruined my harvest! I will lose a week's pay." The distracted soldiers laughed.

"Go on, old man. You are lucky we did not put a blade through you."

The farmer wasted no time. "Hee yah!" he commanded the bullocks, desperate to put distance between the cart and the soldiers. Hee yung Kim pressed hard on his wound, trying to stop the rapid flow of blood. He sighed with relief as he felt the cart sway and move forward. Perhaps the load under him would contain the blood. The cart inched forward.

"Look!" The younger soldier pointed to the pattern of dark spots glaringly clear on the dirt road, whitened by a bright, full moon. "Halt!" The two soldiers sprang forward. They flung burlap bags out of the cart. They saw the black hair of Hee yung Kim. They grabbed him by the shoulders, pulled him from the cart, and dropped him into the dirt. Hee yung Kim groaned aloud with pain and tried to hobble to his feet. The farmer, unnoticed, walked to the side of the cart. He sensed, miles ago, a hidden core of strength in this seemingly frail boy. He tensed, prepared to move quickly.

His injured leg could not stand his weight and Hee yung Kim hunched on his left leg. The young soldier laughed again, drew his right hand back and prepared to throw a sweeping punch at the boy. He was unaware he had unleashed a fiery, deadly, rage in the helpless victim. Hee yung Kim shifted his body counter clockwise on his one leg, leaned and slipped the vicious swing. His left hand swung from the outside and pushed the soldier's arm into his body. His right hand speared across the path of the hapless punch, and into the soldier's throat. The soldier thrust up with the force of Hee yung Kim's knife hand strike, and then fell onto his back. His larynx crushed.

The older soldier hesitated, shocked by his comrade's defeat. Enraged, he rushed forward, grabbed Hee yung Kim's vest, and lifted his body, prepared to slam it to the ground. The weightless, Hee yung Kim swung his body into the soldier. His lead hand grabbed across and under the arm that clutched his tunic. He wrenched and twisted the arm until the soldier bent forward and down. He released Hee yung Kim's vest. Hee yung Kim thrust his injured leg into a long stance against the soldier, and threw a right ridge-hand strike against the exposed nape. Hee yung Kim stepped back, panting with exertion.

The fallen soldier moaned and placed his hands as if to rise. The farmer stepped in front of the boy, lifted the soldier's own dropped bayonet, and plunged it into his back.

They rolled the two bodies as far as they could into the brush. The motorbikes followed. Hee yung Kim considered riding one of the motorbikes. They were only a few miles from Seoul. "Many soldiers will chase us now. They will overtake this slow cart. I must get the *Sam jang kwae* to the Doseonsa Temple." Hee yung Kim spoke aloud, forgetting that his mission was a great secret.

The farmer shook his head. "A Korean peasant boy riding a Japanese motorbike is surely a target. If we lay in the back of the cart as if resting, the soldiers will motor past us. They won't be looking for these two men until they fail to return from their patrol."

Hee yung Kim thought for a moment. Then, he heard the sound of distant trucks, traveling fast, shifting noisily as they made turns. He ran into the brush, righted a motorbike, and pushed it to the road.

"What are you doing?" The farmer turned around. He was quickly tossing the thrown contents back on the cart.

"You are right!" Hee yung Kim yelled to the astounded farmer. "I will be the target. I must be seen going around your innocent cart and fleeing from them." He reached beneath his jacket and untied the cloth belting his wide trousers. He loosened the leather pouch containing the *kwae* . "I already feel weakened from loss of blood, and I cannot take the chance of failing my mission."

Hee yung Kim thrust the leather pouch at the farmer.

"There is a statue of supreme importance in this pouch. You must, I beg you, deliver this statue to the Doseonsa temple. The temple lies at the foot of Mt. Sangaksan. You must, please, make sure Buddhist Acharya receives the statue."

Dim lights broke a distant rise and engine noises grew louder. They looked back toward the oncoming vehicles, and then at each other. "Why is a single statue so valuable?" the farmer asked, as he dutifully tied the pouch within the folds of his trousers.

"It is not the statue that is valuable. The statue contains an object essential to the spiritual and cultural destiny of Korea." He thought of Master Kija. "The protection of the *Taegeuk* is worth lives." Hee yung Kim jumped on the motorbike and furiously pumped the foot pedal. The engine caught and he took off, only to circle back after a few feet. "I almost forgot." He yelled over the engine. "Code word at the gate is Jinul." He turned again and sped away.

The farmer climbed up to the bench seat and adjusted his clothes carefully. He watched the tiny red taillight flicker as Hee yung Kim's motorbike bounced further away. He clucked at the bullocks and they slowly shuffled forward. Suddenly, the Japanese trucks rumbled by, one after another, forcing the farmer to edge far to the side of the road. Clouds of choking dust obscured his view, and caused the bullocks to stamp and shake their heads. He gazed through the brownish haze. "That boy will be surely caught, and tortured to reveal other rebels. Then, he will be imprisoned, or shot."

He urged the animals forward. He knew, well, the

location of Doseonsa Temple. He also knew the Buddhist monk, Acharya. He was eager to tell him about courageous boy saint, Hee yung Kim.

진 Sa-JANG
JIN
THUNDER

Sa Jang is Jin, or thunder, which signifies courage and power. The kwae for Sa Jang consists of two broken lines atop a solid line. Characteristics of thunder are great roars and blasts of power. The solid line shows the courage and perseverance that anchors the sound.

Chin Ho and *O jang*
Eui sook and Sa jang

As the sun rose the next day, Chin Ho and Eui sook, each exhausted, boarded a second train many miles south of Seoul. This old, dilapidated train did not seem capable of holding the many Koreans and Japanese clambering aboard, much less delivering them any distance. Chin Ho and Eui sook were able to grab one seat for the two of them to share. For many miles, they took turns, one sitting and one clinging to a leather loop hanging down from the roof of the car. Conversations swirled, competing with the noise of the train. Master Kija's students, silently, either slumped in a seat, or clung to the loop.

The train stopped at a station near the crest of the mountain city of Taejon. The tone of conversations in their car changed. It seems this was not a usual stop. The riders anxiously craned out the windows.

"It is Japanese checkpoint!" Chin Ho overheard a Korean man croak nervously. He leaned over Eui sook to peer out the grimy window. He gasped. Twenty or thirty Japanese soldiers stood along the wooden station platform. Rifles with fixed bayonets placed in uni-

O-JANG
SEON
WIND

손

Oh Jang is Seon, or wind. Seon represents the paradox of air, or stillness, and wind, or great movement. Its kwae consists of two straight lines atop a broken line, and is directly across Sa Jang on the yin/yang circle. This alignment of lines reflect the weakness and strength inherent in all things.

form precision in front of each soldier. While Chin Ho watched, two soldiers boarded each car of the train.

"They are looking for Korean rebels." An old woman volunteered. Chin Ho and Eui sook froze. The papers that Master Kija prepared allowed them passage on three instances. Although, Chin Ho's heart sank each time he presented them to soldiers. However, the fearful murmurs of fellow passengers signaled danger to both children. Eui sook barely breathed as she watched the armed soldiers approach each of the passengers.

"Why are you here?" the soldier demanded of the tall Korean boy. "You should be in the Emperor's service."

Chin Ho dumbly handed the soldiers his papers.

"Why are you escorting this unworthy girl? You should be serving the Emperor of Japan." He insisted. Eui sook shrank into the seat, as far from the soldier as possible. Chin Ho finally managed a squeaky, "I am her only rel… ."

"Shut up!" He gestured through the window. Two more soldiers climbed into the car. Two of them grabbed Chin Ho's arms. Chin Ho reflectively struggled to free himself, and then stopped. He realized the futility of fighting the soldiers. What would become of Eui sook? He stopped too late. His trouser leg was wrenched aside, and the leather pouch swung heavily against the guard's leg.

"What is this?" The soldier ripped the pouch from Chin Ho's belt. He opened it wide and removed the statue. Gold patina, ruby and emerald gems gleamed. The soldiers were transfixed. Chin Ho thought, he could escape at that moment. No, Eui sook sat, trapped, behind the soldiers. The first soldier pulled Eui sook from her seat, pinned her against his body, and fumbled under her garment for her pouch. A second statue was revealed.

"They are thieves!" the guards announced in unison. They quickly bound the hands of each thief. The soldiers shoved them from the car. "Lock them in the mail car. We must take them into Taejon, where there is a jail. The Commandant will want to interview them. We caught three rebels in a day and night."

Alarmed, Eui sook looked a question at Chin Ho. Who is the third rebel?

Chin Ho whispered. "Let them believe we are only thieves. We do not want them to open the statues."

They mounted the mail car. The guards pushed them to the back, and chained them to an iron rail on the back wall. They threw both pouches into a small, padlocked cupboard. The children watched the soldiers leap from the mail car, slam the outer door, and latch it.

"They do believe we are thieves," Eui sook hissed. "They are not curious about the statues."

"We are still bound." Chin Ho replied. "The statues are still locked up in that cupboard."

"Chin Ho, we are not helpless." Eui sook pulled at the chains. "We have special training, and the power of the *kwaes*. Remember the words of Master Kija. My *Taegeuk kwae* is *Sa jang,* which is *Jin*, or thunder. I can summon power and courage. Most important, according to Master Kija, is the strength of perseverance."

She shook Chin Ho's arm. "Your *Taegeuk O Jang* is

Seon, or air. I do not quite understand it. *Seon* is a paradox. Air is powerful when still, and a mighty wind is powerful. You will utilize the power of *Seon*. I will be *Jin*, thunder. We must act now!" She sat up and pulled at the chain.

"We are locked to an iron rail on a moving train," Chin Ho replied. "How am I supposed to use air to break free?"

"You are not remembering your *poomse*, Chin Ho. Think about the pattern of your form." Eui sook looked carefully at the iron bolt to which chained her to the wall. She gripped the underside of the huge bolt with her left hand. She reached across her left arm and grabbed the top of the bolt with her right hand. She twisted the bolt toward the left, in a crossed grip. The bolt shrieked against the wooden wall. Eui sook pushed her right foot against the wall, twisted and pulled on the bolt. It screeched from the wall.

They quickly looked at the door. No one rushed in. "They did not hear," Chin Ho said with relief. He quickly grabbed his bolt and applied the same pattern. With chains and hooks dangling from their wrists, they turned to the cupboard containing their pouches. The cupboard was midway, under the row of mail sorters. Without hesitation, Chin Ho lunged into a long forward stance, slammed his right elbow into the door, shattering it to pieces. They snatched their pouches and retied them under their trousers.

"Shall I shatter the door?" Chin Ho asked, emboldened by his success with the cupboard door.

"No!" Eui sook said adamantly. They must believe

we are still captive. We will go out the window."

Chin Ho looked at the small, square window. He opened the glass and hoisted himself through the window. His legs dangled inside the car. His top half hung over a rushing blur of rocks. The chain and bolt danced above the moving ground. He was afraid it would catch on something and drag him from the window. Painfully, he turned his body and wedged, sitting up, facing the exterior of the car. He reached up, clutched the overhang of the rail car, and pulled himself up. He lay on top of the car, spent.

"Hurry, haul me up!" Eui sook demanded. He peered over the rail. Eui sook was already braced in the window. He pulled her up. They sprawled on the roof, gasping for breath.

"We are right behind the engine car." She panted. "We must break into that car."

He grouched. "You sound as if it is easy." He looked over the gap between the two cars. There was room to stand, and a ladder welded on the front of the car. They clambered down the ladder. Eui sook was wrong. A coal car followed the engine. Chin Ho winced, grabbed the back gate, and hoisted himself over the edge. He landed on the coals and grunted, "Ouch. These coals are hard as rocks." He crawled forward, getting blacker with each movement. Eui sook followed him.

Once again, they climbed down the metal ladder and onto a narrow platform. Now, they were behind the engine car. Chin Ho grasped a latch on the right side of the engine. Eui sook seized the left hand hold. On a count of three, they each swung the heavy bolts out wide and whipped them into the engine windows. Eui sook jumped onto a small running board, reached through the shattered glass, and opened the door. The shocked rail man pushed at her chest to throw her off the train. Eui sook leaned into his body, swung her right hand high over his left arm and delivered a vicious knife hand strike to his neck. She encircled his right arm above the elbow, twisted her body to the right, and shoved him backwards through the open door.

The engineer on the left rose up and attempted to kick Chin Ho from the running board. Chin Ho quickly wedged himself under the engineer. The engineer was literally sitting in Chin Ho's lap. Chin Ho drew his knees up and twisted his body to the left. The engineer screamed as he ejected from the train. Chin Ho grabbed the door and slammed it shut. Panting, he leaned back onto the seat. He looked over at Eui sook. She shook her head. "I can't believe we were able to do that!"

"You ranted about our amazing power." He retorted. "How will we run this engine?" He studied the unfamiliar array of knobs and dials.

"The Japanese saw the men fall from the train. They are coming!" Eui sook screamed over the rumble of the engines. "They will jump on top of the train like we did."

"We are trapped again," Chin Ho screamed back. "We cannot fight a bunch of them."

Eui sook thought hard. "I know. We wait until they are on top of the train and moving to the engine. Then, we stop the train, instantly."

"I do not know how to stop the train."

Again, he searched the front panel, frantic to find a lever or knob that might stop the train.

"It must be that large lever," Eui sook pointed. "Wait until they are on top of the train."

Soon, they heard thumping on the roofs of the cars. Eui sook looked out her window to see the moving shadows of many soldiers coming towards them. When they reached the roof of the mail car, she shouted. "Now!"

Chin Ho pressed the lever down. The train seemed to fly along the rails even faster. Eui sook could see shadows of the soldiers crouched near the ladder and gap behind the engine. Chin Ho released the lever, waited a second, and pushed it as hard as he could. Another second went by. One of the soldiers descended the ladder and stood behind the engine. A second soldier started down the ladder. Suddenly the brakes seized. The train wheels protested with loud screeches, and the train cars shuttered.

The soldiers atop the cars reeled and waved their arms, and many fell off the cars. A few soldiers threw themselves prone and clung to the roofs. The impetus of the slowing train impelled them forward, out of control. The two soldiers directly behind the engine car were able to brace themselves securely.

The train finally stopped. The screams of jumbled and frightened passengers rang over the hushed train. Chin Ho and Eui sook each braced against the doors. They saw the soldiers approaching on either side of the car. Eui sook shoved her door open, leaned out, and threw the chained bolt at the soldier clinging to the handhold. He grunted in pain, and attempted to bring his rifle into position. Eui sook swung again and her bolt smashed into the soldier's hand, causing him to drop the rifle. As she drew her arm back to swing again, the soldier jumped to the ground and ran.

Chin Ho stepped from the car. He hung onto the doorframe with his left hand, swung his right leg out and kicked his attacker off the train. Chin Ho, now on the small platform behind the engine, thought grimly. "A hundred bullets will rain down on my head."

Eui sook jumped onto the platform. "We must try to uncouple the engine from the rest of the train. Chin Ho, "she shouted. "Jump on that iron tongue and force the hitch down." Chin Ho looked at the iron thing. He jumped heavily on it. Nothing happened.

"Get back inside the engine and figure out how to get it going again." She complied. Once her slight weight left the platform, Chin Ho pushed down on the tongue again. The tongue slipped from the platform and the engine moved an inch. He clambered back into the engine. Eui sook was pushing on a lever.

"I think this is a gear." She gasped. Chin Ho began pushing and pulling at every lever within reach. He could see movement in the side mirror. The soldiers were carefully edging toward the car. Suddenly, the engine huffed and jerked upward. Both children held their breath, and waited to see what would happen next.

"I think we are moving." Eui sook whispered. "Yes! We are moving." The engine car slid along the track at an imperceptive pace.

Chin Ho warned. "We are not going fast enough." The lead soldiers could see that the engine was moving. They rushed forward. Just then, the engine huffed again and jumped forward. It gathered speed and descended a long mountain slope. Ping, ping, ping. A barrage of bullets thumped the back of the engine, as the soldiers, with raised rifles, watched them race out of range.

The engine sped faster and faster and miles lengthened between the car and the soldiers. Eui sook clung to the door. Chin Ho stared out the front window as trees whipped past. He saw the track rise up in the distance. He looked behind the seat. A few black fragments littered the empty coal bin. "We will not be able to go up that hill." He said.

"What hill? Oh no!" she cried, and looked out the window. The track seemed to circle back over them. He nodded. "It is all right. We ran out of coal anyway. The engine will slide back to the bottom of the hill and stop. The Japanese must be a couple miles back. We will jump from the train when it stops and run for the forest. I see smoke over there. That might be the village of Chonju."

"You don't have your papers anymore. What will we do?" Eui sook whimpered, no longer sounding decisive as she did when they were locked up. Chin ho looked at the exhausted girl and realized the next decisions would have to come from him. "First, we must get to that village."

Deng Min and Dang Sun, the Rescuers

As soon as the Engine rolled to a complete stop, Chin Ho and Eui sook jumped down and ran into the forest. Now their fortunes changed, due to the boldness of an elderly Korean woodsman, named Deng Min. Deng Min lived in the tiny village of Nanson, on the southern side of the forests around Chonju. He spent many days in the forests, gathering wood for fuel for his village and for the numerous ferries and small boats on the ports of the Yellow Sea.

On this day, the old man was working close to the rail line, an area he usually avoided because of the heavy Japanese presence. It was near the end of his workday, when the weary Deng Min heard the screeching of metal wheels over the blows of his axe on the logs. He heard the gunfire. He recognized what these sounds meant. "Again," he thought. "Soldiers are chasing some poor wretch." The woodsman stooped down, gathered his wood, and hastened to his cart. He hitched up his nag and waited. Gnarled and scruffy, Deng Min looked incapable of quick thought or courageous deed. In fact, he, and his lifelong friend on the seashore, worked in tandem on many occasions to help lost or fleeing Koreans.

By now the angered soldiers had come upon the empty engine car. They sent for reinforcements from the town of Taejon. The soldiers from the train sought to recover from the humiliation of allowing mere children not only escape, but also disrupt a whole train. They convinced the incoming soldiers that the two captives were not just thieves. "They must be part of the rebel bands from the North," they yelled at the new soldiers. Soon, more than a hundred soldiers were charging noisily through the forest. They spanned out in the dense growth, looking for the thieves/rebels in vain.

Ragged and completely blackened by the coal, the children were virtually invisible as they slipped through the forest brush. The keen eyed Deng Min spotted the two children. He beckoned them to his cart of wood. They collapsed on the logs. He threw a tarp over them, climbed up and gathered his reins, and drove a weaving path through the forest to his home of Nanson. As the nag plodded through the small town, Deng Min jumped from the cart, ducked into a small hut, grabbed a wicker bag filled with provisions, hobbled after the nag, and climbed back on the cart. The children never moved. The horse never stopped.

A day later, the cart and its cargo arrived at Gunsan, on the shore of the Yellow Sea. Deng Min waved to his friend, Dang Sun, sitting on the roof of his small ferryboat. The ferry was attached to a dilapidated pier. Dang Sun spotted the dirty urchins huddling under the tarp and immediately grasped their plight. The two old men quickly hustled the children into the lower quarters of the ferry.

An hour later, a scrubbed and dripping Chin Ho bent over a clay bowl of fish and rice. It was his second bowl. Eui sook ate one bowlful, crawled to a pad in the corner and fell asleep. Dang Sun had run out of his supply of traditional clothes, and both children were dressed in long tunics, over fitted pants. They each wore a woven basket-like pouch tied by a strong sash and strung over one shoulder to the opposite hip. Chin Ho has already placed the statue containing *O Jang* lie in in his basket pouch. Eui sook's basket and her statue containing *Sa jang* lie side by side, near her outstretched arm.

Deng Min unloaded his cart of wood on to the back of the ferry. He bowed goodbye to his fellow conspirator, Dang Sun, climbed aboard the cart, and turned toward Nanson. The old man felt greatly satisfied. He had saved the Korean children from the soldiers. He did not know that he also helped to achieve a crucial mission.

Dang Sun steered his dilapidated boat south, around the many islands off the coast. He had the entire load of wood from Deng Min's cart. As he did not have to gather fuel at any of the islands, he avoided Japanese checkpoints. Hidden away from suspicious eyes, Chin Ho and Eui sook ate and slept during the entire trip. Dang Sun maneuvered around the large island of Jeju and glided into a small cove. The Haenyeo woman swam out to the boat. She had been anxiously waiting for the children. She was extremely happy that they finally made it to the island.

Yuk-JANG
KAM
WATER

Yuk Jang is Kam, or water. Water is like indomitable spirit. Water can be resisted temporarily, but its incessant flow persists. Flowing water, though soft through one's fingers, can carve canyons into mountains and smooth mountains into dust. Its kwae lies opposite the kwae for Sa Jang, or fire, on the yin/yang circle. The kwae is one solid line embraced by two broken lines like the banks of a river.

Chul Moo and *Yuk jang*

Chul Moo lay on the rocky ground, concealed deep in the brush, for what seemed hours. His heart was still hammering against his chest wall. "Surely the soldiers will come back and try to find me," he thought. He relived the scene. Chang nom Kim jumping in front of the Master. Chang nom Kim shouting for the key to *Chil jang*. Then, astoundingly, the quiet, shy Chang nom Kim viciously attacked the soldiers. He killed at least three! Chul Moo recalled the awful noise as each bullet thudded into the skinny, bespectacled body of his friend. He scrunched tightly into the dirt and squeezed his eyes shut. He did not want to remember the sight of Master Kija and Jung sup Kim, stunned and beaten, brutally forced down the path.

Shuddering in fear, Chul Moo fought back tears. Then it dawned on him. The soldiers had forgotten all about him. The soldiers, faced with by the audacious courage of Chang nom Kim, over reacted. They slammed many bullets into young boy and came close to killing Master Kija and Jung sup Kim also. If, by chance, any one of them looked back up the trail, they would see empty space. Chul Moo had slipped into the brush as soon as the scuffle began. He had failed the Master and his friends. He was a coward! No! It was best that one of them escaped into the brush. Now there was a chance. A chance to do what?

"What can I do?" he anguished. He knew that his thinking process was a little slower than that of his fellow students. As he lay there, he remembered the encouraging patience of Master Kija as they talked about his forms. "He was always so kind to me," thought Chul Moo. "Even when Jung sup Kim and Hyun Cho eclipsed my stolid performances, Master Kija treated me with fairness. Not once did he suggest that I learn faster. Perhaps he realized that although slow, I never forget. If I cannot physically practice, I mentally visualize the correct movements."

Chul Moo huddled in the brush as the sun rose and slowly arced across the sky. He mourned Chang nom Kim. Chang nom Kim was the quietest of Master Kija's class and Chul Moo felt comfortable with him. "Chang nom Kim was like the *Chil Jang kwae*," he recalled. "He was *Gan*, the keeping still. Then BOOM, he became the mountain and saved Master Kija and Jung sup Kim." These thoughts made Chul Moo sleepy and he dozed off and on while *Tae Keon* forms skittered though his head. Then, unbidden, Chul Moo began visualizing *Yuk jang*. In his mind, he became Master Kija, speaking softly to Chul Moo about *Yuk jang*, just as the Master spoke to Jung sup Kim about *Il jang*, and Hyun Cho about *Yi jang*.

"Taegeuk *Yuk Jang* represents *Kam*, which is water. The kwae has a solid line between two broken lines, symbolizing a river between its guarding banks. Wa-

ter is cunning, even devious. Water's unalterable softness will eventually penetrate the densest matter. Water
carves channels through stone. Water is like indomitable spirit, never giving up. Water is relentless!" Chul
Moo jumped up in the dark brush. "I am like flowing water! I am dangerous! He shook his hands at the
heavens. "We are partners, Chang nom Kim and I. I
must complete the mission and save Master Kija and
Jung sup Kim." Then, as in his nature, Chul Moo flung
his body on the rocky ground and determinedly mulled
through a strategy.

The rural Korean house is simple in its construction and built to accommodate the harsh Korean win-
ters. Large boulders anchor each corner of each po-
tential room. Earthen walls are built to the height of
these foundation stones. Rot resistant pine boards line
the earthen walls, and provide a base for a latticed timber construction. Over these timber walls, the families weave a tight, waterproof thatch of rice straw. Most
families reinforce the thatch roofs periodically, increas-
ing the durability of the roofs. Chul Moo concentrated
on the interior two rooms. The floor in the main room
consists of packed mud, over a series of stone lined
channels. Heavy oiled paper lines the packed mud
floor. Koreans do not wear shoes inside, and the floors
remain clean for sleeping and eating. The kitchen room
is lower than the main room and has a beaten smooth
earthen floor. The cooking fireplace on the inner wall of
the kitchen provides heat and hot smoke, which snakes
through the mud covered channels of the main room
and creates an extremely effective radiant heating.

Chul Moo thought about earthen walls, mud floors, and the resolute quality of water. A plan slowly evolved in his mind. Above the village of Sinuju, in the midst of the forest, lies a deep depression in which the yearly melting April snows create a watery expanse. Many years prior, the villagers built an earthen dam on the lower side of the water. The result was a deep pond of fresh water. Chul Moo's heartbeat increased. He got to his feet and slowly crept down the mountainside. The sun was far in the West when he finally reached the edge of Sinuju. "I must find out where the soldiers put Master Kija and Jung sup Kim before dark," he thought desperately.

Chul Moo climbed a tall fir and peered through the dusty needles. Immediately, he focused on a hut somewhat apart from the main village. Two Japanese soldiers were leaning casually against the hut, smoking cigarettes. He almost laughed as he realized that the hut's proximity to the village would ensure that his plan would not harm other structures. Chul Moo scampered down through the rough branches and edged north, careful to remain out of sight of anyone.

When he finally reached the earthen dam, it was darkening. He could see lit cooking fires and smell roasting vegetables far below. Ignoring his rumbling stomach, Chul Moo realized the darkness would actually help him carry out his plan. He searched around and found a stout fallen limb, about six feet in length. He pulled a small pocketknife from the pouch that also contained the *kwae* of *Yuk jang*. He sank cross-legged to the leafy ground and methodically began scraping the end of the limb.

Much later, under the high full moon, Chul Moo moaned aloud in frustration. His raw, bleeding hands throbbed. His sore, bent back would not straighten. Repeatedly, throughout the night, Chul Moo plunged his sharpened branch into the packed earth wall of the dam. Hindered by embedded rocks and limbs, his bludgeoned weapon had penetrated a mere foot. "I'll never breach this dam." He muttered. "How can I save the Master and Jung sup Kim? Think! Think! What would Master Kija do to break through the dam?" Suddenly, Chul Moo straightened as the words sprang from him. "Use the water!"

Quickly, Chul Moo stripped off his vest and trousers. He carefully wrapped his clothes and placed them out of range. He found his knife under the pile of loosened dirt. He placed the knife hasp in his mouth and scampered up the dam, directly over the rough opening. The dark, still water below made him pause slightly. He shrugged off his hesitation and dove straight down. The pond was not deep and he reached the bottom immediately. He whipped around, and plunged his small knife into the muddy wall. He dug for an interminable time, probably two minutes. He sprang up into the night air, gasped great draws of air, and forced his tiring body down again. He lost count of the frantic dives. He became water in his mind. Relentlessly, he drove his knife through the mud, reaching dry earth, until his hand and knife became lost in the watery hole. Exhaustion overcame him. After several tries, he was able to launch up and over the ledge. Fearfully, he stretched his neck and peered down through the darkness.

"There!" He inhaled deeply. "What is that?" The silver moon reflected a small slender band coming from the outside crack. Chul Moo jumped down and felt the ground beneath the orifice. "Wet! Water!" Weariness banished, he watched the little stream broaden. Suddenly, he realized he had more work to do. He shoved dirt, branches, and rocks, this way and that, creating a shallow trench to direct the water on a straight path to the back wall of the hut. The wonderful stream silently flowed toward the dirt foundation. The two guards would not hear or see the watery attack. The breach grew bigger and the stream strengthened. Chul Moo recovered his clothes and the pouch and put his knife away. He quietly followed the stream downward to begin the next phase.

The Rescue of Jung sup Kim and Master Kija

Jung sup Kim awoke suddenly, his heart racing. "What is it?" he thought. He looked at Master Kija, who seemed to have entered into some sort of trance. He lay tightly, painfully, trussed. His chest was barely moving. His eyelids were relaxed and closed. On the other hand, Jung sup Kim's whole body pulsed with tension, and he quickly rose to his feet. He felt the quietness of night, but there was something else. A small, unfamiliar noise persisted. He thought it might be the guards, shuffling cards or whispering. He pressed his eye against the latticed wood, but could only see the downturned head of one guard. He seemed to be asleep.

Jung sup Kim willed his body to still, and relied on his senses of sight and sound. Minutes crawled. He closed his eyes and listened. The same furtive incessant, sound seemed to grow. He opened his eyes and stared through the shadows of the small room. "I must be crazy!" he thought. "I think the wall is moving." He closed his eyes again. Then he reopened them. "The floor is sinking into the rock channels!" He edged toward Master Kija, as if to protect him.

Suddenly, the wall seemed to burp loudly. Two mud-encased sticks protruded the belching wall and clawed at the room. Jung sup Kim yelped and almost jumped on top of Master Kija. Master Kija's eyes flew open. They both stared at the wall. Jung sup Kim trembled with fear. Master Kija could only move his eyes. The clawing sticks lunged into the room, followed by a ghastly figure, sheathed in mud and spurting blood.

"Arrgh!" A tremendous gush of watery mud engulfed the figure, as the wall broke open behind him. Only when the muck began to dissolve from the figure, did the two shocked prisoners realize that it was a tall boy. And the tall boy was Chul Moo

"My knife!" Chul Moo said, and tossed the muddy blade to a stunned Jung sup Kim. "Quickly free Master Kija. I am sure the guards are alerted." In fact, they could hear the guards beating on the door. The mud and debris released by the water settled on the far wall and partially blocked the door. Once released, Master Kija could not immediately move his frozen muscles. Jung sup Kim had no time to wonder at this new Chul Moo, one who broke through walls. The two boys grabbed each other's hands, whipped their arms under Master Kija and carried him between them. They struggled frantically against the rising debris, stumbling on the slippery stones of the floor channels. The unleashed might of the water now worked against them. They forced themselves through the dilapidating wall, desperately dragging Master Kija, now each with one arm. They realized that the Master was in great pain, but they could not stop until free of the sludge. Finally, the two boys slogged to the edge of Chul Moo's trench, and literally launched Master Kija over the brink and out of the current. They each rolled over the side and sprawled helplessly near the Master.

Jung sup Kim could hear the shouts and commands of the melee around the hut. "The soldiers will quickly figure out that we are not in the debris of the hut and come after us." It made no difference. He could not move yet. He managed to turn his head and found Chul Moo, almost invisible among the bushes. He, too, was unmoving except for dragging in great breaths of air.

Within seconds of each other, Jung sup Kim and Chul Moo crawled to the inert Master. He was covered in muck, and Chul Moo wiped his face as clear as possible. Master Kija opened his eyes and looked at Chul Moo for many seconds as if seeing a mirage. Slowly, he moved his head from side to side. He lifted his arms gingerly and looked at his unsteady hands, wavering in front of Chul Moo's face.

"Chul Moo!" He whispered hoarsely. "I never doubted your courage! I never.." he coughed and groaned aloud with the movement of his body. "I always believe…" he began again but could not finish. Chul Moo shook his head. "No, Master. It was I who doubted me. I know that now. He put his long arms around Master Kija and attempted to help him to a sitting position. Master Kija groaned again. His old body had been severely stressed. "The action of Chang nom Kim finally made me realize we each will find the strength, the will." Chul Moo could not continue either, and tears crumpled his sad, muddy face.

Jung sup Kim was a few feet away, rocking on his hands and knees. He raised his head and looked around. "We must hurry! All the soldiers will come after us now, and surely will kill us." He crawled over to them. Master Kija was moaning softly. Chul Moo's body was shaking with the effort to restrain his sobs. "I don't think he can be moved!"

"We must. There is no choice. We will be seen at any time. We must move or be killed!" Jung sup Kim raised to his knees and moved to the other side of the Master. He placed his arms around the Master's back and under his knees. "Chul Moo, we can carry him as before." Chul Moo nodded and bent to grasp the other side of the Master. Jung sup Kim could barely stifle his tears as Master Kija gasped aloud with the pain caused by their efforts.

"I'm so sorry Master," he grunted. "We have to get to the forest." They stumbled through the brush, intent on reaching the safety of the dark forest. Chul Moo slipped on loose rocks and they went down in a heap of muddy arms and legs.

"Pull me into that copse of trees just over there," Master Kija weakly instructed. "I won't be able to go further, but you must. I need to talk to you."

"That's not far enough!" Jung sup Kim shouted. The boys hefted the Master over their crossed arms again and staggered over the rocky ground. Master Kija was thin and frail, but the boys each realized they would barely reach the copse before collapsing. This final exertion sent them crashing down between the trees, slamming Master Kija to the ground on his back. "Oomph!"

He grunted.

"I am so sorry," moaned Jung sup Kim. "I could not hold on a bit longer." Chul Moo inexplicably burst into tears again.

"Tut!" Master Kija whispered. "Brace me against the big fir tree. I have much to say."

The boys rose tiredly and pulled Master Kija through the thick debris. Inured now to his moans, they propped him against the fat trunk and collapsed beside him. They were somewhat hidden, now in the thick stand of trees and brush.   For many minutes the escapees sat silently, each thinking, in his own way, about their dilemma.

It dawned on Jung sup Kim that they need not worry about noises they made while dragging Master Kija to the copse. The deafening clamber of the soldiers eclipsed any sounds in the small copse. Villagers were also running frantically around, trying to salvage their threatened huts. Chul Moo's trench had collapsed and the little river became a wide, muddy expanse, threatening much of Sinuju. The soldiers were in a complete uproar, shouting mindless orders, and roughly handling the villagers, as they looked for the escaped prisoners.

Master Kija was quite still, with his eyes closed. Suddenly, his eyelids folded up and his black eyes became large in his old, shriveled face. "The boys, his brave boys, must escape, " he realized. He raised his palm; effectively silencing the whimpering Chul Moo. "Chul Moo," he began in a thin, shaky voice. "Have you lost the *yuk jang kwae*?" Chul Moo started, jumped to his feet and madly pawed through his muddy trousers.

"No, no. I can feel the statute!" He wrenched the pouch from his waist. It was wet, filthy, and held fast by the strong cord to his belt. "Master Kija, I used its power. I remembered all the *taegeuk*. That is how I created the river which breached the walls."

"Excellent, excellent," breathed Master Kija. He straightened and said in a surprisingly strong voice. "Now, the two of you have the most dangerous errand possible. You must find where the Japanese have *Il jang* and *Chil jang*. *Il jang* was ripped from Jung up Kim when they tossed us in the hut. *Chil jang* may be hidden in the trousers of Chang nom Kim."

"You mean, uh on his body?"

"Yes, the soldiers probably tossed him aside, not believing the ragged young boy would have anything of value. You must find both of these *kwaes* and deliver them to the destinations we talked about."

Chul Moo again sank to his knees beside Jung sup Kim, who said tremulously, "I am not sure I remember my destination. I am so sorry. I do remember I was to go to the south."

"Yes. You become a laborer on a fishing vessel that docks at the Port of Pohang. A Taigu monk will meet you there. I suspect the monks are extremely worried as they expected you days ago. The monk will take you to the city of Daegu. I told you of the Buddhist Monk, Woncheuk, who lives and works in the Taigu Temple. He will care for you and the *Il jang kwae*. First, you must find *Il jang*!"

Master Kija leaned back against the trunk, closed his eyes again, and struggled to gain the strength to finish his desperate instructions. The tired boys looked at each other in wonderment. How did the Taigu monks expect Jung sup Kim?

"Another thing!" Chul Moo jumped a foot. Jung sup Kim whipped around at Master Kija's outburst.

"Chang nom Kim was to deliver *Chil jang* to the Haedong Yonggung Temple in Pusan. This is a famous temple sitting on the coast of the Korean Strait. The ocean washes right up the stones of the temple and there are various tombs deep in the temple caverns. Jung sup Kim, you can deliver *Chil jang* to the temple. A young Buddhist monk, Gihwa, is awaiting Chang nom Kim."

"Master, how can I be in two places?" interrupted Jung sup Kim. "It is amazing," he thought silently. "This frail, exhausted old man has, once again, become a warrior, armed with a multitude of complex details. He leans helplessly against a tree trunk and infuses us with indomitable spirit."

Master Kija did not answer, but instead continued. "Buddhist Woncheuk will summon the young Gihwa to meet you at the Taigu temple and retrieve *Chil Jang*. There is a railroad, the Gyeongbu Line, which connects Seoul and Pusan. The railroad passes through Daegu. The monk, Gihwa, will come as student to Buddhist Woncheuk. Then Gihwa will return on the train to Pusan. He will hide *Chil jang* deep in the caverns of the Haedong Yonggung Temple. Yes. That will work."

The uproar in the village had died down somewhat. Chul Moo scampered up a tall fir and surveyed the mess that had once been an orderly village. The soldiers seemed to be no longer in complete pandemonium. They were gathering in groups, and Major Yamagata was shouting orders. He hurried to the ground. "I think the soldiers are organizing search parties. We must move deeper into the forest."

"No." Master Kija replied. "You must listen and not speak. I will be captured." He tried to wriggle to a less painful position, but gave up. The boys were shocked into silence.

Master Kija stoically swallowed his pain and cleared his face. " I still have much to tell you. I must be captured," he repeated. "You both must escape and complete your mission.

"No! No!" wailed Chul Moo. Jung sup Kim remained passive. He realized minutes ago, when Master Kija was telling them what to do, that this was the only possible outcome if the *Taeguek* Circle was to be saved.

"Yes," Master Kija responded firmly. "While the soldiers are applauding my capture, the two of you will find the body of Chang nom Kim. *Chil jang* is in the folds of his garments. Then you must retrieve *Il jang*. The village is still in chaos, but the statue is guarded, I am sure. You will have to handle that." Master Kija's voice faded to a forced whisper.

"Please, let us save you!" Chul Moo pleaded.

"Tut!" The soldiers will not kill me. The Japanese Emperor greatly desires the *Taegeuk* Circle. He wants the power of 'Yadool'. He believes he can wield its manifest power. The soldiers will hold me until the Emperor's special soldiers arrive. "

"Chul Moo, return to our *dojang* on the mountain. The soldiers did not find our cave in which *Pol jang* remains hidden.   Tend to the pigeons. New birds will have arrived. I know you have watched me wrap the coded words to their legs. You will live in the cave and communicate with our friends. You must now provide care and learning for the young villagers. When you are fully grown, you will become the Master of the *dojang* of Mount Paektu."

Chul Moo leaned to the Master to hear his faltering words. "Chul Moo, there are many rebels hiding in the forests around our mountain. They will provide pro-tection for you. Now, go, go fast. Obey me in this. You have the future of Chosen in your hands."

Jung sup Kim was busy clearing debris and bushes aside to provide a path. He did not want Master Kija to remain in the woods unattended. "Hopefully, Master Kija is correct and the soldiers will not harm him." He muttered.

"Go, Go. Obey my instructions!" Master Kija's last woods boomed from his frail body.

Chul Moo
and Jung sup Kim escape

"This way, there are foot prints here!" The soldiers were nearing.

Jung sup Kim whipped by Chul Moo and ran deeper into the woods. Chul Moo followed more slowly. "I am desolate," he whispered. "I cannot leave Master Kija, and yet I know I must. My head is reeling."

Jung sup Kim had disappeared. Chul Moo melted into the woods a second before the soldiers came upon the prone Master Kija. The boys ran south through the trees, then turned to the west and entered Sinuju. They were not recognized. Everyone in the village was ragged and covered in mud. The villagers valiantly tried to stem the water and save the dirt foundations of their homes.

"One can hardly tell the difference between the villagers and the Japanese soldiers," Jung sup Kim shouted to Chul Moo. Chul Moo nodded. He felt a tinge of pride that his plan had worked to this extreme. Pride quickly faded to shame as he watched the men, women and children trying to save their humble homes.

He bumped into Jung sup Kim. "What do you see?"

The older boy pointed. Chul Moo squinted, but did not understand what Jung sup Kim was seeing.

"Look, there in the mule's stable behind the hut of Dae Ho." Jung sup Kim began to run.

Chul Moo followed closely. The stable was three sided with the south side open and strewn with hay. They now recognized three ragged covered bodies, carelessly thrown into the stable. One was Chang nom Kim. They stopped, horrified, but neither made a sound. Jung sup Kim quickly rifled through the voluminous trouser folds of his dead friend and tore the pouch free. He felt the bulge of the statue and did not wait to open the pouch. Chul Moo leaned over Chang nom Kim, brushed leaves from his face, found his cloth square each of them wore under their vests, and covered his face. "Let us find *Il jang!*"

Minutes later, they notice a relatively clean Japanese soldier standing next to a small, unoccupied hut. "He must be guarding the statue. Only one guard, but he is that giant, Sergeant Yui."

Chul Moo also remembered Sergeant Yui, and he immediately devised a plan. "We will separate and come at the guard from both sides. I will make a noise so he starts toward me. When his back is turned, you attack. When he turns toward you, I will attack. We will pull his body into the hut and retrieve *Il jang*. We have to be quick, before anyone notices."

Chul Moo's plan worked. Each of them bolstered with new strength born of vengeance for their dead friend.

Master Kija

Jung sup Kim and Chul Moo fled up the slope of Mount Paektu to the trailhead of their familiar path. There, they solemnly saluted each other in the fashion of the *Tae Keon.*

"*Keom sa mi da,* dear friend," said Chul Moo. I know you will be safe on your travels. Have a good life in the Taigu Temple. We will talk through our carrier pigeons."

"*Keom sa mi da,*" Jung sup Kim answered. He turned and hustled down the path leading south.

Chul Moo began his trek up the well-known trail, his mind whirling with emotions and thoughts for the future.

At first, the soldiers thought they found Master Kija's dead body. One of the guards kicked at his ribs, and the old man grunted. "He's alive!"

"Good," a second soldier said. "We will teach him to escape. Enough torture and he will reveal where the boy is."

The soldiers half-carried, half-dragged Master Kija through the mud and brush. The chaos abated slightly in Sinuju, but both villagers and soldiers were busy trying to restore some sort of order. The only structure standing relatively free of both mud and workers was the small hut where they had thrown the pouch.

"Where is that fat, lazy guard?" The soldiers paused, and Master Kija slid to the ground. "Well we can throw this old man inside. He will not be able to free himself. He is practically dead. Open the door."

Major Yamagata commanded the door to be opened. A young soldier dashed forward and pushed at the door. "It will not open." Another soldier put his shoulder against the door and the two pushed as hard as they could. They shoved violently, and the door actually broke into pieces. "It is Yui!" Pieces of the door covered the body of the large guard. Chul Moo and Jung sup Kim had rolled the body into the hut and the body rolled back against the door when it shut.

"Bind this old fool from head to foot and throw him into the hut," barked the frustrated Major. We must find those demons before they harm another valiant soldier."

For three days, Master Kija lay tightly bound on the floor of the hut. Villagers could see him through the shattered door, but none of them dared to offer water or food. Meanwhile, the enraged Japanese thrashed through the forests around Sinuju. The soldiers followed one futile lead after another. Just as Master Kija foretold the boys, revolutionaries hiding in the forests placed many false clues, leading the search parties away from Mount Paektu and the fleeing boys.

The frustrated Japanese dragged Master Kija from the hut, unbound him, and lashed him to a bare sapling. The soldiers took turns beating him with sticks, and his bloody body slumped closer to the ground. He was near death.

The water ebbed into scattered pools and no longer threatened what was left of earthen foundations. The bright noon sun slowly dried the ground. Many of the Sinuju villagers and their children huddled in their collapsed homes, unwilling to watch the destruction of Master Kija. Others could not look away, and tears ran down sad faces.

The soldiers stopped the beating, believing that the old man must surely die soon. Silence clamped down on the unmoving figures, soldiers and villagers. The noon sun beat down on the tragic tableau. Suddenly, Master Kija planted his feet beneath him and slowly straightened against the sapling. Everyone was spellbound. They watched a virtual reincarnation as the bloodied old man tilted his head upward and opened his eyes. There! Nearly invisible in the glare of the sun, a small bird, wings spread wide, soared across the sky. To everyone's astonishment, a tiny smile altered the bloodied face. Then, he closed his eyes, but still stood tall and straight.

Skidding tires and grinding gears speared through the silence. A canvas topped military lorry sped into the village clearing. A high-ranking soldier, with the insignia of a Colonel jumped from the vehicle.

"Who is in charge?" He demanded.

Major Shiho Yamagata stepped forward and saluted. "I am in charge. We have captured a leader of the rebels. He refuses to answer any questions. He and his cohorts are responsible for the destruction of this village and the death of some of my men. We will soon capture his followers, as they are young, unworthy boys."

"Where is the *Tae Keon* Master Kija who trains in the forests around Mount Paektu?"

Startled, Major Yamagata turned slowly and pointed to the bound prisoner. "That is the *Tae Keon* Master. He has caused much trouble for my soldiers."

"No! He cannot die. I am Colonel Kimura of the Japanese Imperial Army stationed in Seoul. Governor General Masatake has directly ordered me to take Master Kija into custody."

"He is captured! We are grilling him for information. His followers have killed many of my soldiers." Major Yamagata appeared agitated and just a little fearful in front of the villagers.

"Grilling? You are grilling him? Your men are beating him to death." Colonel Kimura took a step back as if to broaden his audience and reinforce his rank. " Japanese Emperor Hirohita is sending a contingent to Seoul to arrest this *Tae Keon* Master and immediately transport him to Tokyo. You must unbind him, cleanse him, and make sure he has food and water. If he dies, you and everyone of your soldiers will suffer the consequences."

The soldiers untied Master Kija and carried him to the hut. Two of the village women rushed in with wet cloths and blotted the blood from his body carefully. A small girl followed with some rice water and a bowl of kimchi. Two soldiers stood in the doorway among the shattered wood and watched every move. Master Kija seemed to be revived somewhat with the rice water, but declined the kimchi.

"I will return in one hour with my men. They are twenty or thirty kilometers from here." Colonel Kimura said. "Ring the hut with your soldiers, Major Yamagata. They are to stand, shoulder to shoulder, tight against the hut, and stay vigilant. Extremely vigilant! These people appear to be worried about this old man."

"Remember. The Emperor wants this man alive!" Colonel Kimura jumped into his lorry and sped out of Sinuju.

The major's men complied and lined themselves tightly around the small hut. Major Yamagata commandeered a keg from nearby, and sat, facing the spectacle. "All this for a frail, beaten, old man," he muttered.

A little more than an hour later, Colonel Kimura drove sedately into the clearing. His men trotted, tiredly behind the Colonel's vehicle. A large canvas roofed truck followed the men, presumably with other officers inside.

Major Yamagata still sat on the keg, facing the hut. His men were still tightly gathered around the four walls.

"Back the truck toward the hut," commanded Colonel Kimura. "The old man will need to lie down. He nodded to Major Yamagata. "I brought a surgeon to attend to the aged gentleman."

Major Yamagata simply shrugged and motioned for the two guards in front of the door to move aside. All the other soldiers remained in place.

Colonel Kimura walked importantly to the hut and entered. Immediately, he flew out. "What the devil is this?" he roared.

"What?" Major Yamagata hurried to the door and peered in. On the floor inside lay a kimchi filled bowl and an empty cup. That was all. Master Kija had vanished.

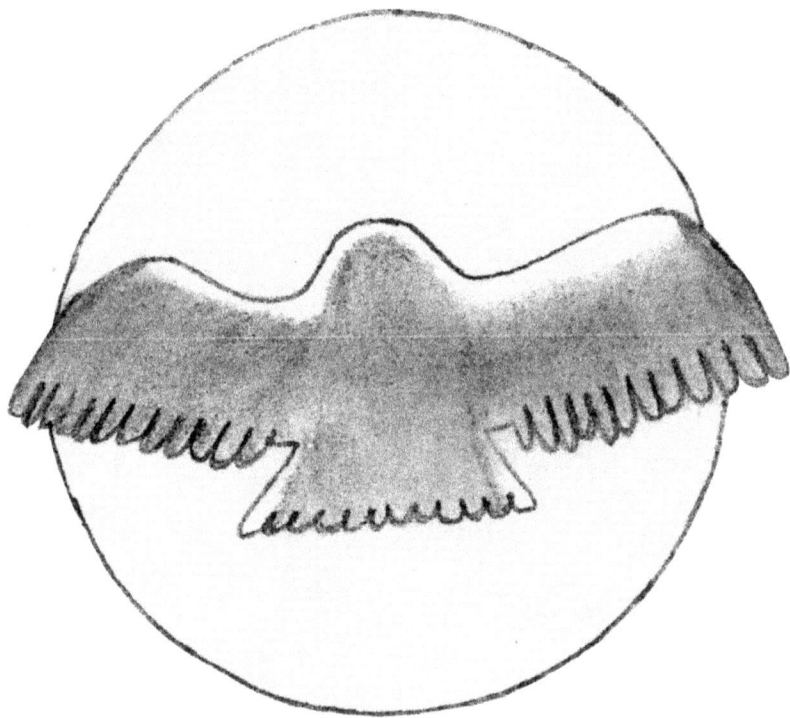

EPILOGUE – 1945

Eui Sook and *Sa Jang* – Chin Ho and *O jang*

Eui sook dove into the cold blue water with a small splash and speared toward the ocean bed. It was a good day. The war was ending. She already gathered three giant abalones this morning. The brilliant sunshine lit the water and exposed every species of seafood with great clarity. Eui sook was one of the more famous Haenyeo on the island of Jeju. Traditional Haenyeo women are stocky and squat in nature. Although powerful as her peers, Eui sook was tall and lithe. She was especially happy today. The war was ending. Soon, she would hear from Master Chul Moo.

Eui sook's husband, Chin Ho would sail into harbor tonight with his ocean bounty of deep-sea tuna. He would be thrilled, also, about the closing of the horrible war and the end of Japanese occupation. Now, he too, would await a message from Master Chul Moo with feverish anticipation.

Hyun Cho and *Yi Jang*

Hyun Cho kicked debris viciously and the racket echoed throughout the large domed structure. He studied the broken windows; bullet ravished walls, and blackened beams. "Yes, it will work." He said to the walls. This old building will again become a great sanctuary. This building will be a haven for all those in need. He thought lovingly of Chin Mae, who died, nearly one hundred years old, in the last month. She had worked tirelessly with Hyun Cho to retrieve ownership of the Jinheung sanctuary. A tribute to the good man Dongsun will hang in the apse.

Master Chul Moo's carrier pigeon arrived earlier in the month. "Continue your work in Hungnam," the Master insisted. We will know when to make further plans."

Hee yung Kim and *Sam Jang*

Hee yung Kim sprawled on the small, flat bow of the ferryboat that once belonged to Dang Sun, and now belonged to his grandson, Deng Sun. Now a middle-aged man, Hee yung Kim still suffered ill health effects after his years in the Japanese prison camp. Always a courageous man, Hee yung Kim successfully planned and executed a mass escape for many of the young and weakest in the camp in the year 1925. Again, he created a diversion by heading south, drawing the Japanese guards away from the weakened escapees. His name is famous throughout the Korean peninsula for his legendary, self-sacrificing exploits. A tribute to Hee yung Kim hung prominently in the Doseonsa Temple on the outskirts of Seoul.

When Hee yung Kim escaped south, he fled through same dark forest near the small town of Nanson in which the old woodsman, Deng Min lived. Although ninety years old, Deng Min effortlessly whisked Hee yung Kim to safety in the same cart that once held Eui sook and Chin Ho. Deng Min, and his equally ageless friend, Dang Sun, had continued to save many fleeing orphans and other refuges throughout the occupation. Hee yung Kim was severely ill and near death when Deng Min found him, and brought him to the port of Gunsan.

Hee yung Kim spent his days idly. He fished with Deng Sun, and entertained the children of Gunsan. Nothing really changed his life as the war ended. "Some day," he thought, "I'll venture back to Sinuju. I wonder if Chul Moo is running the *dojang*? Somehow, I believe he is following in Master Kija's footsteps."

Jung sup Kim and *Il Jang*

Master Jung sup Kim watched proudly as his young students performed their poomses. He was especially glad today because the air was light with freedom. The *Tae Keon* students no longer have to practice in secret in the Taigu Temple. Master Kim was renowned in the city of Daegu, and throughout Korea, for his organization of martial arts classes during the Japanese occupation. No more secrecy. His students would no more furtively dash through the streets of his own city. Master Kim was in regular communication with Master Chul Moo on Mount Paektu. They would soon devise another essential plan for the future of Korea

Buddhist Monk Gihwa and *Chil Jang*

Buddhist Gihwa, a wrinkled brown old man, sat against the warm stones of the Haedong Yonggung

Temple and let the gentle waves of the Korean strait lap against his sandaled feet. He was content. The Japanese occupation was over. Relief swept over him. He no longer need fear a sudden search and seizure operation by Japanese soldiers. The secret of the *Chil Jang* will remain so. Soon, Master Chul Moo will communicate with him.

Master Chul Moo in Sinuju

The occupation was over. Master Chul Moo content-edly watched his students draw on great sheets of rice paper. They were planning a new *dojang*. The *dojang* would be a grand building of stone, erected above the village of Sinuju on the southern slopes of Mount Paek-tu. A small separate temple will be constructed on an adjacent meadow. The body of Chang nom Kim will be interred in the temple. His likeness, painted on the temple wall, will shine with great reverence.

"One day," Master Chul Moo mused, "I will retrieve Pol Jang from the cavern. Unification of the Taegeuk Circle is inevitable. Korea's national spirit will live un-der the protection of the Taegeuk Circle.

ABOUT THE AUTHOR
HARTLEY BIO

Master Hartley was introduced to the Martial Art discipline of Taekwondo when she ferried her grandchildren to the Big Sky dojang and sat through their classes three days a week. As a retired history instructor she was drawn to the culture and ethos of Korean martial arts. As a lifelong jogger, she craved a renewed gratification of physical exertion. She joined a beginning class and the martial arts culture claimed a major role in her life.

When she earned her first Black Belt, Grandmaster Noyes and Master Noyes offered her the chance to help instruct Taekwondo classes. She continues to teach and is grateful to work with the gifted young instructors of Big Sky Martial Arts and the aspiring athletes. Master Hartley also referees in Montana tournaments, which allows her edifying interaction with other dojangs and students.

She calls herself a "perennial" student and earned

her Fourth Degree Black Belt in 2014. Her little story, "Yadool", fulfills an ardent desire to enlighten students and interested persons to the enriching Taekwondo principles and spirit.

www.ingramcontent.com/pod-product-compliance
Lightning Source LLC
Chambersburg PA
CBHW071001040426
42443CB00007B/601